PRIMARY

comprehension

C

Fiction and nonfiction texts

Published by Prim-Ed Publishing

www.prim-ed.com

6255C

PRIMARY COMPREHENSION *(Book C)*

Published by Prim-Ed Publishing 2006
Reprinted under licence by Prim-Ed Publishing 2006
Copyright© R.I.C. Publications® 2005
ISBN 1-84654-010-0
PR–6255

Additional titles available in this series:
PRIMARY COMPREHENSION *(Book A)*
PRIMARY COMPREHENSION *(Book B)*
PRIMARY COMPREHENSION *(Book D)*
PRIMARY COMPREHENSION *(Book E)*
PRIMARY COMPREHENSION *(Book F)*
PRIMARY COMPREHENSION *(Book G)*

Internet websites
In some cases, websites or specific URLs may be recommended. While these are checked and rechecked at the time of publication, the publisher has no control over any subsequent changes which may be made to webpages. It is *strongly* recommended that the class teacher checks *all* URLs before allowing students to access them.

View all pages online

Website: www.prim-ed.com

Email: sales@prim-ed.com

PRIMARY COMPREHENSION

Foreword

Primary comprehension is a series of seven books designed to provide opportunities for pupils to read texts in a variety of fiction, poetry and nonfiction genres, to answer questions at literal, deductive and evaluative levels and to practise a variety of selected comprehension strategies.

Titles in this series include:

- *Primary Comprehension* Book A
- *Primary Comprehension* Book B
- *Primary Comprehension* Book C
- *Primary Comprehension* Book D
- *Primary Comprehension* Book E
- *Primary Comprehension* Book F
- *Primary Comprehension* Book G

Contents

TEACHERS NOTES

Twenty different texts from a variety of genres are given. These include humour, fantasy, a myth/legend, folktale, mystery, adventure, horror/supernatural, fairytale, play, fable, science fiction, poetry and informational texts/nonfiction such as a diary, report, biography, newspaper article, letter, procedure, diagram and a film review.

Three levels of questions are used to indicate the reader's comprehension of each text.

One or more particular comprehension strategies has been chosen for practice with each text.

Each text is given over four pages. Each group of four pages consists of:

~ a teachers page

~ pupil page – 1   (which always includes the text and sometimes literal questions)

~ pupil page – 2   (which gives literal, deductive and evaluative questions)

~ pupil page – 3   (which concentrates on the chosen comprehension strategy/ strategies)

Teachers page

The **title of the text** is given.

Question types and comprehension strategies refer to the three levels of questioning and any particular strategies used.

The particular text **genre** is given.

Worksheet information details any background information required by the teacher about the genre or subject of the text or specific details regarding the use of the worksheets.

Answers are always given for literal questions and for deductive questions where appropriate. Answers for evaluative questions are best checked by the teacher following, or in conjunction with, class discussion.

Extension activities suggest titles of books or authors who write in the same genre, as well as other literacy activities relating to the text.

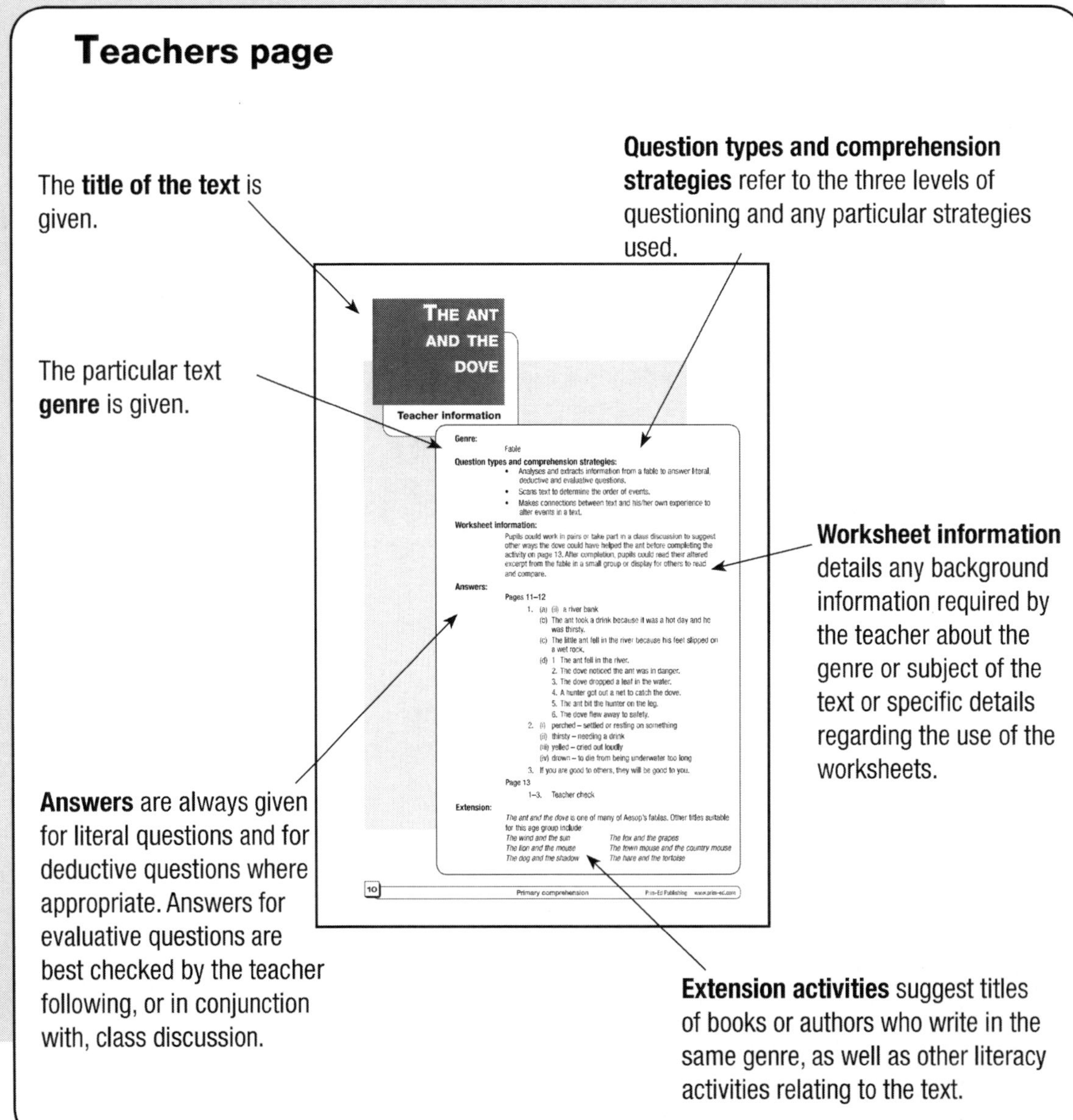

Teachers Notes

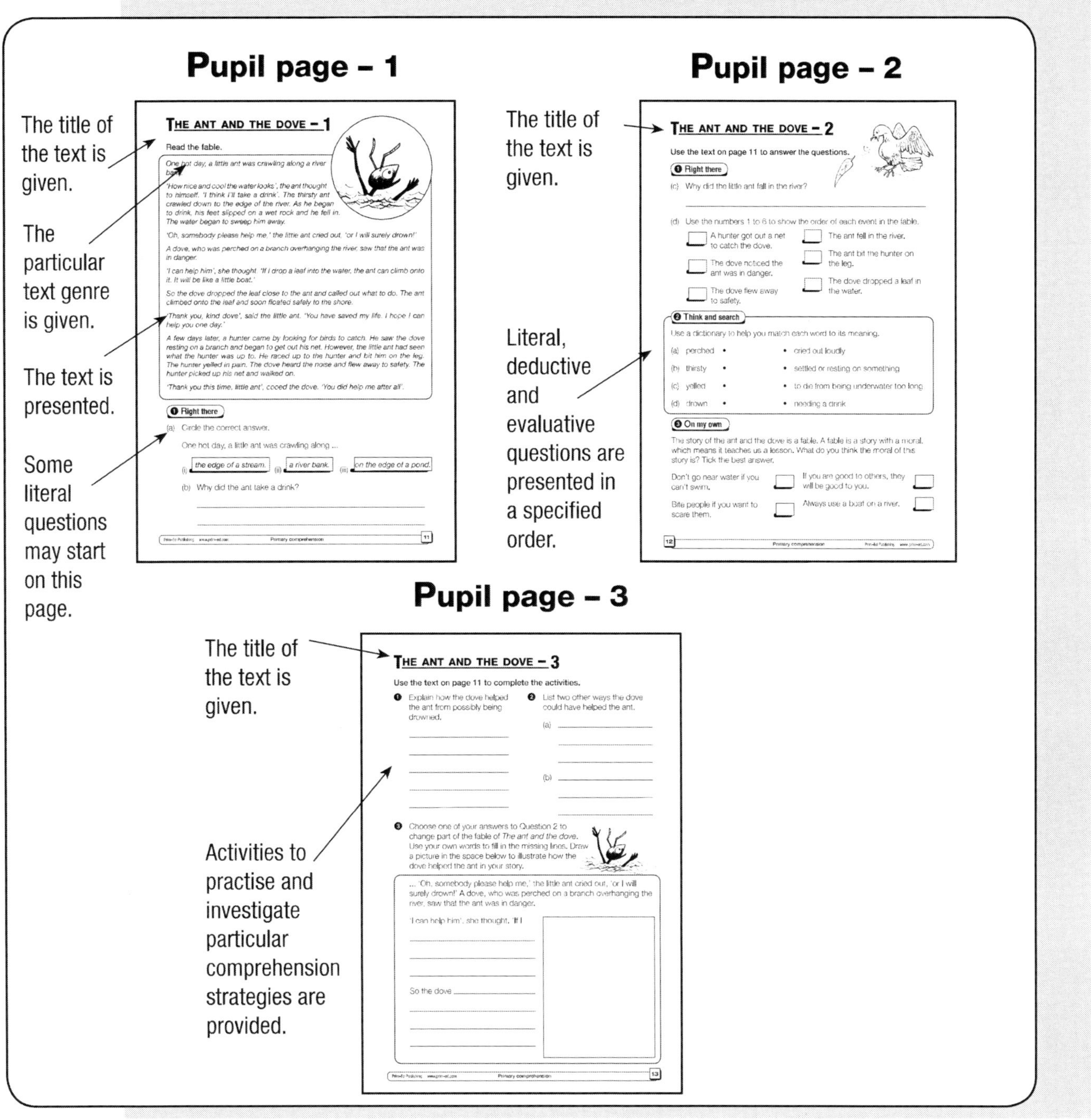

Types of questions

Pupils are given **three types (or levels) of questions** to assess their comprehension of a particular text in each genre:

- **Literal questions ('Right there')** are those which can be found directly in the text. These come first in the questions and are grouped.
- **Deductive (or inferential) questions ('Think and search')** follow the literal questions. Deductive questions are implied in the text and require the reader to read between the lines and think a bit more deeply about what has just been read.
- **Evaluative (or response/applied) questions ('On my own')** require the reader to think even further about the text and incorporate his/her personal experiences and knowledge to answer.

Answers for literal questions are always given and may be found on the teachers page. Answers for deductive questions are given where appropriate. Evaluative questions are best checked by the teacher following, or in conjunction with, class discussion.

Comprehension strategies

Reading comprehension is an essential part of the reading process. Pupils need to comprehend what they read in order to become fluent readers.

The teacher is crucial in teaching and encouraging the use of comprehension strategies. Pupils' comprehension improves when teachers provide explicit instruction in comprehension strategies and when they implement activities that provide opportunities to practise and understand these strategies.

Several specific comprehension strategies have been selected for practice in this book.

Although specific examples have been selected, often other strategies, such as scanning, are used in conjunction with those indicated, even though they may not be stated. Rarely does a reader use a single strategy to comprehend a text.

Strategy definitions

Predicting

Prediction involves the pupils using illustrations, text or background knowledge to help them construct meaning. Pupils might predict what texts could be about, what could happen or how characters could act or react. Prediction may occur before, during and after reading, and can be adjusted during reading.

Pages 2–5, 6–9, 34–37, 38–41, 42–45, 70–73 and 74–77 use the strategy of predicting.

Making connections

Pupils comprehend texts by linking their prior knowledge and the new information given in the text. Pupils may make connections between the text and themselves, between the new text and other texts previously read, and between the text and the world.

Pages 6–9, 10–13, 14–17, 22–25 and 46–49 use the strategy of making connections.

Comparing

This strategy is closely linked to the strategy of making connections. Pupils make comparisons by thinking more specifically about the similarities and differences between the connections being made.

Pages 18–21, 22–25, 26–29 and 58–61 use the strategy of comparing.

Sensory imaging

Sensory imaging involves pupils utilising all five senses to create mental images of passages in the text. Pupils use visual, auditory, olfactory, kinaesthetic or emotional images as well as their personal experiences to create these images. The images may help them to make predictions, form conclusions, interpret information and remember details.

Pages 2–5, 30–33, 34–37, 38–41, 42–45 and 78–81 use the strategy of sensory imaging.

Determining importance

The strategy of determining importance is particularly helpful when pupils are trying to comprehend informational texts. It involves pupils determining the important theme or main idea of particular paragraphs or passages.

As pupils become effective readers, they will constantly ask themselves what is most important in a phrase, sentence, paragraph, chapter or whole text. To determine importance, pupils will need to use a variety of information, such as the purpose for reading, their knowledge of the topic, background experiences and beliefs, and understanding of the text format.

Pages 18–21, 46–49 and 50–53 use the strategy of determining importance.

TEACHERS **NOTES**

Skimming	Skimming is the strategy of looking quickly through texts to gain a general impression or overview of the content. Readers often use this strategy to quickly assess whether a text, or part of it, will meet their purpose. Because this book deals predominantly with comprehension *after* reading, skimming has not been included as one of the major strategies.
Scanning	Scanning is the strategy of quickly locating specific details such as dates, places or names, or those parts of the text which support a particular point of view. Scanning is often used but not specifically mentioned when used in conjunction with other strategies.

Pages 10–13, 30–33, 42–45, 50–53, 54–57, 58–61, 62–65, 66–69 and 78–81 use the strategy of scanning.

Synthesising

Synthesising is the strategy which enables pupils to collate a range of information from a variety of sources in order to comprehend texts. Pupils recall information, order details and piece information together to make sense of the texts. Synthesising helps pupils to continually monitor their understanding of the text. Synthesising involves connecting, comparing, determining importance, posing questions and creating images.

Pages 14–17, 26–29, 54–57, 62–65, 66–69 and 70–73 use the strategy of synthesising.

Paraphrasing/Summarising

Summarising involves the processes of recording key ideas, main points or the most important information from a text. Summarising or paraphrasing reduces a larger piece of text to the most important details.

Pages 38–41, 50–53, 58–61, 74–77 and 78–81 use the strategy of summarising/paraphrasing.

Shared and guided reading

Reading comprehension needs to be taught if pupils are to learn how to understand and engage with texts. The structure of comprehension lessons needs to provide direct teaching on the application of reading comprehension strategies.

Shared reading

To introduce the lesson, the teacher models reading the text, including a demonstration of how to use the comprehension strategies required by the specific unit of work. The demonstration might include:
- linking information in new text to prior knowledge
- generating mental images of parts of text
- asking 'why' questions
- pausing during reading and asking predictive questions

or any of the strategies outlined on pages vi and vii.

Guided reading

The pupils work in groups to complete the comprehension activities. The teacher works with and supports the pupils, prompting them to use different strategies to solve the questions; for example, the strategy modelled in the shared reading session should be applied to the text.

Plenary

Comprehension lessons should be concluded using a plenary session, giving the teacher and pupils the opportunity to discuss a range of issues, including:
- re-emphasis and practise of strategies
- clarification of misconceptions
- reflection and personal response
- explanation of how pupils solved particular questions
- presentation and discussion of work

Genre definitions

Fiction and poetry

Science fiction
These stories include backgrounds or plots based upon possible technology or inventions, experimental medicine, life in the future, environments drastically changed, alien races, space travel, gene engineering, dimensional portals or changed scientific principles. Science fiction encourages readers to suspend some of their disbelief and examine alternate possibilities.

Horror/Supernatural
Stories of this type are those which aim to make the reader feel fear, disgust or horror. A number of horror stories have become classics. These include *Frankenstein* by Mary Shelley, *Dracula* by Bram Stoker and *Dr Jekyll and Mr Hyde* by Robert Louis Stevenson.

Mystery stories
Stories of this kind focus on suspense and the solving of a mystery. Plots of mysteries often revolve around a crime, such as murder, theft or kidnapping. The hero must solve the mystery, overcoming unusual events, threats, assaults and often unknown forces or enemies. Stories about detectives, police, private investigators, amateur sleuths, spies, thrillers and courtroom dramas usually fall into this genre.

Fables
A fable is a short story which states a moral. Fables often use talking animals or animated objects as the main characters. The interaction of the animals or animated objects reveals general truths about human nature.

Fairytales
These tales are usually about elves, dragons, hobgoblins, sprites or magical beings and are often set in the distant past. Fairytales usually begin with the phrase 'Once upon a time ...' and end with the words ' ... and they lived happily ever after'. Charms, disguises and talking animals may also appear in fairytales.

Fantasy
A fantasy may be any text or story which is removed from reality. Stories may be set in nonexistent worlds such as an elf kingdom, on another planet or in alternate versions of the known world. The characters may not be human (dragons, trolls etc.) or may be humans who interact with non-human characters.

Folktales
Stories which have been passed from one generation to the next by word of mouth rather than being written down are folktales. Folktales may include sayings, superstitions, social rituals, legends or lore about the weather, animals or plants.

Plays
Plays are specific pieces of drama, usually enacted on a stage by a number of actors dressed in make-up and appropriate costumes.

Adventure stories
Exciting events and actions feature in these stories. Character development, themes or symbolism are not as important as the actions or events in an adventure story.

Humour
Humour involves characters or events which promote laughter, pleasure or humour in the reader.

Poetry
This is a genre which utilises rhythmic patterns of language. The patterns include meter (high and low stressed syllables), syllabification (the number of syllables in each line), rhyme, alliteration, or a combination of these. Poems often use figurative language.

Myths
These are stories which explain a belief, practice or natural phenomenon and usually involve gods, demons or supernatural beings. A myth does not necessarily have a basis in fact or a natural explanation.

Legends
Legends are told as though the events were actual historical events. Legends may or may not be based on an elaborated version of an historical event. Legends are usually about human beings, although gods may intervene in some way throughout the story.

TEACHERS NOTES

Genre definitions

Nonfiction

Reports

Reports are written documents describing the findings of an individual or group. They may take the form of a newspaper report, sports or police report, or a report about an animal, person or object.

Biographies

An account of a person's life written by another person is a biography. The biography may be about the life of a celebrity or a historical figure.

Reviews

A review is a concise summary or critical evaluation of a text, event, object or phenomenon. A review may give a perspective, argument or purpose. It offers critical assessment of content, effectiveness, noteworthy features and often ends with a suggestion of audience appreciation.

Letters

These are written conversations sent from one person to another. Letters usually begin with a greeting, contain the information to be related and conclude with a farewell signed by the sender.

Procedures

Procedures are instructions which tell how to make or do something. They use clear, concise language and command verbs. A list of materials required to complete the procedure is included and the instructions are set out in easy-to-follow steps.

Diaries

A diary contains a description of daily events in a person's life.

Other **informational texts** such as **timetables** are excellent sources to teach and assess comprehension skills. Highly visual texts such as diagrams have been included because they provide the reader with other comprehension cues and are less reliant on word recognition.

CURRICULUM LINKS

England Literacy Year 3

Texts — Objectives

Objectives	The amazing adventure Pages 2–5	A DVD dimension Pages 6–9	The ant and the dove Pages 10–13	King Arthur Pages 14–17	Gavin, the gentle giant Pages 18–21	Beatrix Potter Pages 22–25	Two letters Pages 26–29	Cirrus the centaur's show Pages 30–33	Don't you dare tell Pages 34–37	The marshes Pages 38–41	Remote control Pages 42–45	The school play Pages 46–49	From the cow to you Pages 50–53	How to make slime Pages 54–57	April fool! Pages 58–61	Jojo, the monkey Pages 62–65	Giant butterfly Pages 66–69	Dinosaur find? Pages 70–73	Diary of an ant Pages 74–77	Halvar's house Pages 78–81
Term 1																				
• Read a range of fiction and poetry:																				
– stories with familiar settings															•					
– plays												•								
• Read a range of nonfiction:																				
– information texts on topics of interest													•							
– reports						•					•						•	•		
• Text level work:																				
– read playscripts												•								
– recognise key differences between prose and playscript												•								
– express their views about a story															•					
– write simple playscripts based on reading												•								
– read information passages and identify main points/gist of text						•					•		•				•	•		
– make record of information from texts read						•							•				•	•		
– write simple non chronological reports from known information																	•			
Term 2																				
• Read a range of fiction and poetry:																				
– legends				•																
– fables			•																	
– traditional stories					•			•												•
• Read a range of nonfiction:																				
– instructions														•						
• Text level work:																				
– identify typical story themes			•																	
– identify and discuss main characters and evaluate their behaviour				•	•			•												•
– describe and sequence key incidents in a variety of ways			•																	•
– write alternative sequels to stories			•																	
– read and follow simple instructions														•						
– write instructions, using writing frame														•						

CURRICULUM LINKS

England   Literacy Year 3

Texts

Objectives		The amazing adventure (2–5)	A DVD dimension (6–9)	The ant and the dove (10–13)	King Arthur (14–17)	Gavin, the gentle giant (18–21)	Beatrix Potter (22–25)	Two letters (26–29)	Cirrus the centaur's show (30–33)	Don't you dare tell (34–37)	The marshes (38–41)	Remote control (42–45)	The school play (46–49)	From the cow to you (50–53)	How to make slime (54–57)	April fool! (58–61)	Jojo, the monkey (62–65)	Giant butterfly (66–69)	Dinosaur find? (70–73)	Diary of an ant (74–77)	Halvar's house (78–81)
Term 3	**Read a range of fiction and poetry:**																				
	– adventure and mystery stories	•	•							•	•										
	– humorous poetry															•					
	Read a range of nonfiction:																				
	– letters written for range of purposes							•													
	Text level work:																				
	– retell main points of story in sequence																			•	
	– refer to significant aspects of the text and know how language is used to create these	•	•																		
	– discuss characters' feelings, behaviour and relationships	•	•							•	•									•	
	– read poetry that entertains																•				
	– recognise rhyme that creates effects																•				
	– plot a sequence of episodes modelled on a known story	•	•							•										•	
	– write poetry that has distinctive rhyme																•				
	– read examples of letters written for a range of purposes							•													

Northern Ireland   English (Reading) Year 4

		The amazing adventure (2–5)	A DVD dimension (6–9)	The ant and the dove (10–13)	King Arthur (14–17)	Gavin, the gentle giant (18–21)	Beatrix Potter (22–25)	Two letters (26–29)	Cirrus the centaur's show (30–33)	Don't you dare tell (34–37)	The marshes (38–41)	Remote control (42–45)	The school play (46–49)	From the cow to you (50–53)	How to make slime (54–57)	April fool! (58–61)	Jojo, the monkey (62–65)	Giant butterfly (66–69)	Dinosaur find? (70–73)	Diary of an ant (74–77)	Halvar's house (78–81)
Range	**engage with a range of texts, including:**																				
	– stories	•	•	•	•	•			•	•	•						•			•	•
	– poems																		•		
	– plays												•								
	– informational materials						•	•				•		•	•			•	•		
	– visual materials													•							
Purpose	**read for information**	•	•	•	•	•	•	•	•	•	•	•	•	•	•	•	•	•	•	•	•
Reading activities	**take part in shared reading experiences**	•	•	•	•	•	•	•	•	•	•	•	•	•	•	•	•	•	•	•	•
	retell/reread poems or stories			•			•	•				•		•	•		•			•	•
Expected outcomes	**begin to use evidence from the text to support their views**	•	•	•	•	•	•	•	•	•	•	•	•	•	•	•	•	•	•	•	•
	show understanding of ways texts are structured	•			•			•				•	•				•	•	•		•
	collect information relevant to specific purposes and represent their findings in a variety of ways	•	•	•	•	•	•	•	•	•	•	•	•	•	•	•	•	•	•	•	•
	read a wide range of texts independently and discuss what has been read	•	•	•	•	•	•	•	•	•	•	•	•	•	•	•	•	•	•	•	•

Primary comprehension   Prim-Ed Publishing   www.prim-ed.com

CURRICULUM LINKS

Republic of Ireland — English Language (Reading) — 2nd Class

Texts / Objectives

Objective	The amazing adventure (2–5)	A DVD dimension (6–9)	The ant and the dove (10–13)	King Arthur (14–17)	Gavin, the gentle giant (18–21)	Beatrix Potter (22–25)	Two letters (26–29)	Cirrus the centaur's show (30–33)	Don't you dare tell (34–37)	The marshes (38–41)
Receptiveness to language — experience the reading process being modelled	●	●	●	●	●	●	●	●	●	●
engage in shared reading activities	●	●	●	●	●	●	●	●	●	●
develop reading skills through engaging with appropriate reading material	●	●	●	●	●	●	●	●	●	●
adapt reading style for different purposes	●	●	●	●	●	●	●	●	●	●
Competence and confidence — perform simple information retrieval tasks	●	●	●	●	●	●	●	●	●	●
Developing cognitive abilities — develop comprehension strategies	●	●	●	●	●	●	●	●	●	●
predict future events and outcomes	●	●							●	●
Emotional and imaginative development — engage with a wide variety of text	●	●	●	●	●	●	●	●	●	●
respond to characters and events in a story	●	●	●	●	●			●	●	●
explore different attitudes and feelings by imagining what it would be like to be certain characters	●	●		●	●			●	●	●

Objective	Remote control (42–45)	The school play (46–49)	From the cow to you (50–53)	How to make slime (54–57)	April fool! (58–61)	Jojo, the monkey (62–65)	Giant butterfly (66–69)	Dinosaur find? (70–73)	Diary of an ant (74–77)	Halvar's house (78–81)
Receptiveness to language — experience the reading process being modelled	●	●	●	●	●	●	●	●	●	●
engage in shared reading activities	●	●	●	●	●	●	●	●	●	●
develop reading skills through engaging with appropriate reading material	●	●	●	●	●	●	●	●	●	●
adapt reading style for different purposes	●	●	●	●	●	●	●	●	●	●
Competence and confidence — perform simple information retrieval tasks	●	●	●	●	●	●	●	●	●	●
Developing cognitive abilities — develop comprehension strategies	●	●	●	●	●	●	●	●	●	●
predict future events and outcomes	●							●	●	●
Emotional and imaginative development — engage with a wide variety of text	●	●	●	●	●	●	●	●	●	●
respond to characters and events in a story					●				●	●
explore different attitudes and feelings by imagining what it would be like to be certain characters	●	●			●	●				●

Scotland — English Language (Reading) — Primary 4

Level B

Objective	The amazing adventure (2–5)	A DVD dimension (6–9)	The ant and the dove (10–13)	King Arthur (14–17)	Gavin, the gentle giant (18–21)	Beatrix Potter (22–25)	Two letters (26–29)	Cirrus the centaur's show (30–33)	Don't you dare tell (34–37)	The marshes (38–41)
Reading for information: look at texts with a practical purpose							●			
use wide selection of informational text									●	●
Reading for enjoyment: experience fiction and poems with a variety of styles	●	●	●	●	●			●	●	●
Reading to reflect on the writer's ideas and craft: predict events	●	●						●	●	●
answer questions	●	●	●	●	●	●	●	●	●	●
recall and refer to own experiences		●			●	●			●	●
sequence thoughts and ideas	●	●	●				●			
respond through drawings and diagrams			●	●	●	●			●	
Knowledge about language: discuss characters and scenes in fiction	●	●	●		●			●	●	●
encounter poems										

Objective	Remote control (42–45)	The school play (46–49)	From the cow to you (50–53)	How to make slime (54–57)	April fool! (58–61)	Jojo, the monkey (62–65)	Giant butterfly (66–69)	Dinosaur find? (70–73)	Diary of an ant (74–77)	Halvar's house (78–81)
Reading for information: look at texts with a practical purpose	●		●	●				●		●
use wide selection of informational text			●	●				●	●	
Reading for enjoyment: experience fiction and poems with a variety of styles		●			●	●				●
Reading to reflect on the writer's ideas and craft: predict events								●	●	●
answer questions	●	●	●	●	●	●	●	●	●	●
recall and refer to own experiences				●	●	●			●	●
sequence thoughts and ideas	●	●	●	●	●		●		●	●
respond through drawings and diagrams			●	●		●			●	●
Knowledge about language: discuss characters and scenes in fiction		●			●	●			●	●
encounter poems						●				

CURRICULUM LINKS

Scotland
English Language (Reading)
Primary 4

Texts

Objectives

Objectives	The amazing adventure (Pages 2–5)	A DVD dimension (Pages 6–9)	The ant and the dove (Pages 10–13)	King Arthur (Pages 14–17)	Gavin, the gentle giant (Pages 18–21)	Beatrix Potter (Pages 22–25)	Two letters (Pages 26–29)	Cirrus the centaur's show (Pages 30–33)	Don't you dare tell (Pages 34–37)	The marshes (Pages 38–41)	Remote control (Pages 42–45)	The school play (Pages 46–49)	From the cow to you (Pages 50–53)	How to make slime (Pages 54–57)	April fool! (Pages 58–61)	Jojo, the monkey (Pages 62–65)	Giant butterfly (Pages 66–69)	Dinosaur find? (Pages 70–73)	Diary of an ant (Pages 74–77)	Halvar's house (Pages 78–81)
Level C — Reading for information:																				
– scan for specific information	●	●	●	●	●	●	●	●	●	●	●	●	●	●	●	●	●	●	●	●
– identify the sequence of information			●										●	●	●				●	●
– record information in different ways	●	●	●	●	●	●	●	●	●	●	●	●	●	●	●	●	●	●	●	●
Reading for enjoyment:																				
– identify with characters and comment on their behaviour and reasons	●	●	●	●	●			●	●	●	●	●			●	●			●	●
Reading to reflect on the writer's ideas and craft:																				
– make predictions	●	●						●	●	●								●	●	●
– identify main ideas	●	●	●	●	●	●	●	●	●	●	●	●	●	●	●	●	●	●	●	●
– skim and scan to verify decisions	●	●	●	●	●	●	●	●	●	●	●	●	●	●	●	●	●	●	●	●
– go beyond literal answers to make inferences and conclusions	●	●	●	●	●	●	●	●	●	●	●	●	●	●	●	●	●	●	●	●
Awareness of genre:																				
– adjust reading approaches to the different ways information is presented in different nonfiction texts						●	●						●	●				●	●	
Level D — Reading for information:																				
– complete practical reading tasks														●						
– gather information from a wide range of formats						●	●				●	●	●	●				●	●	
Reading for enjoyment:																				
– become familiar with features of nonfiction texts						●	●						●	●				●	●	
Reading to reflect on the writer's ideas and craft:																				
– study characters, events, conflicts etc.	●	●	●	●	●			●	●	●	●	●				●	●		●	●
– make predictions	●	●						●	●	●								●	●	●
Awareness of genre:																				
– compare texts						●														
– recognise how informational texts differ						●	●				●		●	●				●	●	
– sequence and predict informational texts											●		●	●				●		

Primary comprehension

CURRICULUM LINKS

Wales
English (Reading)
Year 3

	Texts →	The amazing adventure Pages 2–5	A DVD dimension Pages 6–9	The ant and the dove Pages 10–13	King Arthur Pages 14–17	Gavin, the gentle giant Pages 18–21	Beatrix Potter Pages 22–25	Two letters Pages 26–29	Cirrus the centaur's show Pages 30–33	Don't you dare tell Pages 34–37	The marshes Pages 38–41	Remote control Pages 42–45	The school play Pages 46–49	From the cow to you Pages 50–53	How to make slime Pages 54–57	April fool! Pages 58–61	Jojo, the monkey Pages 62–65	Giant butterfly Pages 66–69	Dinosaur find? Pages 70–73	Diary of an ant Pages 74–77	Halvar's house Pages 78–81
Objectives																					
Range:	– develop as independent and reflective readers	●	●	●	●	●	●	●	●	●	●	●	●	●	●	●	●	●	●	●	●
	– read for information, using progressively more challenging texts	●	●	●	●	●	●	●	●	●	●	●	●	●	●	●	●	●	●	●	●
	– participate in independent and shared reading of playscripts												●								
	– read and use a wide range of nonfiction sources of information						●	●						●	●				●	●	
	– read texts with challenging subject matter that extends thinking		●	●					●	●		●	●					●	●		
	– read texts with a variety of structural and organisational features							●					●	●	●				●	●	
	– read modern poetry																●				
	– read texts from a variety of cultures and traditions																				●
	– read myths, legends and traditional stories			●	●	●															
Skills:	– respond imaginatively to plot, characters, ideas, vocabulary and language in literature	●	●	●	●	●			●	●	●	●	●			●	●			●	●
	– use inference and deduction and refer to relevant passages to support their opinions	●	●	●	●	●	●	●	●	●	●	●	●	●	●	●	●	●	●	●	●
	– use prediction	●	●						●	●	●								●	●	●
	– read for different purposes, including skimming, scanning and detailed reading	●	●	●	●	●	●	●	●	●	●	●	●	●	●	●	●	●	●	●	●
	– make succinct notes		●				●	●					●		●		●		●		
	– re-present information in different forms												●		●		●			●	●
Language development:	– recognise the organisational, structural and presentational features of different types of text						●	●				●	●	●	●		●	●	●		

Genre:

Adventure

Question types and comprehension strategies:

- Analyses and extracts information from an adventure narrative to answer literal, deductive and evaluative questions.
- Predicts an alternative ending to a story.
- Uses sensory imaging to describe a setting to create mental images for the reader.

Worksheet information:

Write pupils' suggestions for answers to the questions on page 5 on the board. Explain that keywords and phrases are sufficient. Encourage them to use language that makes the reader feel he/she is in the dungeon.

Answers:

Page 4

1. (a) Because the castle was closed and they could not visit the dungeons which he and Ellen had been looking forward to doing.
   (b) It was the boundary to a maze.
   (c) Choose from: dimly lit, cold, damp, smelled musty, mouldy brick walls
2. (a) (i) quickly   (ii) hurried
   (b) Teacher check
3. Teacher check

Page 5

Teacher check

Extension:

- Research castles, including the main features such as battlements, drawbridges, moats and dungeons.
- Read and make a class list of adventure stories involving castles or mazes; e.g. *The castle in the attic* by Elizabeth Winthrop.

Read the adventure story.

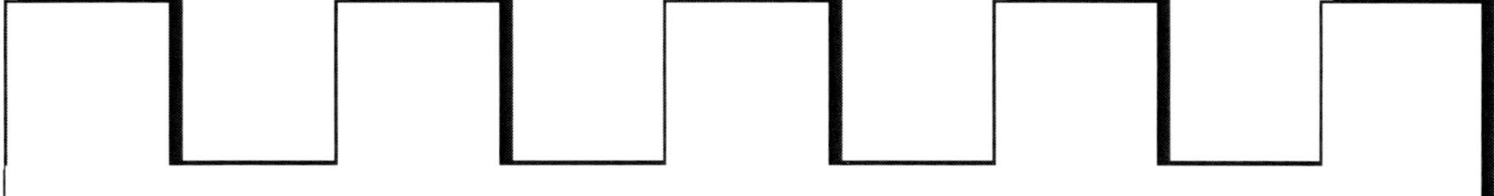

The twins were looking forward to visiting the mysterious castle dungeons. But as they raced to the enormous, thick wooden drawbridge, they saw that the castle was closed. Only the gardens were open to the public.

'Rose beds and daisies!' cried James in disgust. 'Who wants to look round a boring old garden? Ellen! Where are you?'

'Bet you can't find me!' giggled his sister from behind a tall hedge.

James ran to the hedge and, to his delight, discovered that it was the boundary of a maze. He ran in, following the sound of Ellen's laughter. Before long, he was hopelessly lost. He began to panic, but as he turned the next corner, he realised he was at the centre of the maze. On the ground was an open trapdoor which revealed a flight of steps leading down into the darkness.

With his heart thumping loudly, he slowly began to descend. The steps led to a dimly lit passageway. The air felt cold and damp and it smelled musty. Ahead, he could see a shadow dancing on the mouldy brick walls. Ellen!

'Wow! We did get to see the dungeons after all!' squealed James. 'Look at all this stuff! Scary! I don't fancy being stuck in here for long. Let's go!'

James and Ellen hurried back along the passage and up the steps. They were very relieved that the trapdoor was still open.

'Fresh air!' sighed James, taking a deep breath. 'I think I'd like to take a walk around the sweet-smelling rose beds now.'

'Me, too,' agreed Ellen, 'but first we have to get out of this maze!'

THE AMAZING ADVENTURE – 2

Use the text on page 3 to answer the questions.

❶ Right there

(a) Why was James grumpy at the beginning of the story?

____

____

(b) What did James discover about the tall hedge?

____

____

(c) Write three words or phrases from the story which describe the dungeons and passageway.

____

____

____

❷ Think and search

(a) Tick or write the correct answer.

   (i) James and Ellen left the dungeon ...

   slowly ☐   quickly ☐

   (ii) Which word in the story tells you this?

____

(b) (i) Which twin do you think is the more adventurous?

____

   (ii) Why do you believe this?

____

____

____

❸ On my own

James and Ellen wanted to visit the dungeons, yet when they found them, they did not want to stay very long.

Write words and phrases in the boxes to describe a situation that might be both exciting and a little scary.

Situation ____

exciting part	scary part

THE **AMAZING ADVENTURE – 3**

James and Ellen left the dungeon very quickly. How do you think their adventure might have ended if they had explored a little further?

❶ Answer the questions to help you write a plan for a different ending to the story. Use descriptive words and phrases to make the readers feel they really are in the castle dungeon.

(a) Where did they go next?	(b) Were they separated? If so, how did it happen and how did they find each other again?
(c) Did they see any wildlife or other people?	(d) Did they find another way out of the dungeon?
(e) How did they get back to the gardens?	

❷ (a) Use your answers to write a story on another sheet of paper about exploring the dungeon.

(b) Give your story a title.

A DVD DIMENSION

Teacher information

Genre:

Science fiction

Question types and comprehension strategies:

- Analyses and extracts information from a science fiction narrative to answer literal, deductive and evaluative questions.
- Predicts events to complete a story.
- Makes connections between characters in a story and himself/herself.

Worksheet information:

Pupils may complete an ending in a separate writing lesson to show how Carly returns to the video store.

Answers:

Page 8

1. (a) True   (b) False   (c) True   (d) True
2. Answers will vary, but may include:

    (a) ' ... everyone was talking about it so they thought it would be good.'

    (b) ' ... magical and able to transport her into another dimension.'

    (c) ' ... just robbed Sparkles jewellery store.'

    (d) ' ... do karate/defend herself.'

3. Teacher check

Page 9

1–2.   Teacher check

Extension:

Other suggested science fiction titles:

I was a third grade science project by Mary Jane Auch

Akiko on the planet Smoo by Mark Crilley

The transmogrification of Roscoe Wizzle by David Elliott

A DVD DIMENSION – 1

Read the science fiction story.

It was Saturday morning and Carly was at the video store with her mum to choose some DVDs to hire. It was her eighth birthday and her mum had allowed her to invite four friends to sleep over at her house to celebrate.

She already knew one DVD she wanted to choose. Carly and her friends wanted to watch the new film based on a comic book character—'Amazing Girl'. Everyone was talking about it! She walked to the 'New releases' section and quickly scanned the shelves for the title. When she asked the man at the desk, he handed her a copy from a shelf underneath.

'I think that you will really get a kick out of this!' he said with a sly grin.

As Carly took hold of the DVD, a shimmering rainbow light surrounded her. A strong wind lifted her hair and rushed around her body. A buzzing noise filled her ears. Her heart beat rapidly in her chest but she was too scared to even scream.

The light, noise and wind stopped as quickly as they had begun. Carly found herself in a darkened city landscape, wearing a tight pink and green suit with a green cape flowing down her back. Her eyes were shielded by a bright pink mask.

She spun around quickly as she heard a noise behind her. Two masked figures wearing black clothing were running towards her, each carrying a bag labelled 'Sparkles Jewellers'. Sirens and alarms screeched in the background.

'Get out of the way!' yelled the first robber. 'You don't want to mess with us!'

In the blink of an eye, Carly stuck out her foot and brought her hand down sharply on the neck of the first figure. He crumpled to the ground like a marionette who had lost its strings. The second figure stumbled over his companion as he turned his head to see who was following him. The police reached the men as they scrambled to their feet and prepared to flee.

'Great job again, Amazing Girl!' said the police officer. 'It's lucky that you were in the right place at the right time!' He briskly shook Carly by the hand as his men bundled the robbers into a nearby police van.

Carly stared after them in amazement. It had all happened in an instant. How had she managed to stop the robbers? She didn't know how to do karate! And how on earth was she going to get back to the video store? Was she going to miss her own birthday party …?

A DVD DIMENSION – 2

Use the text on page 7 to answer the questions.

❶ Right there

Colour **True** or **False** for each sentence.

(a) Carly was picking out some DVDs for her sleep over.

TRUE
FALSE

(b) Carly was celebrating her seventh birthday.

TRUE
FALSE

(c) 'Amazing Girl' is a DVD based on a comic book character.

TRUE
FALSE

(d) Carly became 'Amazing Girl' and caught the robbers.

TRUE
FALSE

❸ On my own

Use the box to write a sentence or two about a comic book character you would like to be. Explain what this character would be able to do.

❷ Think and search

Complete the sentences.

(a) Carly and her friends wanted to watch the 'Amazing Girl' DVD because

____

____

____

(b) The DVD which Carly touched was

____

____

(c) The two masked men had just

____

____

(d) When Carly transformed into Amazing Girl, she also got the ability to

____

____

A DVD DIMENSION – 3

After reading the text on page 7, complete the following questions.

1 With a partner, discuss how the story should end. List some ideas to show how Carly could get back to the video store in time for her birthday party.

- ____

  ____

- ____

  ____

- ____

  ____

2 Complete the table to compare Carly and yourself.

Similarities	Differences

THE ANT AND THE DOVE

Teacher information

Genre:

Fable

Question types and comprehension strategies:

- Analyses and extracts information from a fable to answer literal, deductive and evaluative questions.
- Scans text to determine the order of events.
- Makes connections between text and his/her own experience to alter events in a text.

Worksheet information:

Pupils could work in pairs or take part in a class discussion to suggest other ways the dove could have helped the ant before completing the activity on page 13. After completion, pupils could read their altered excerpt from the fable in a small group or display for others to read and compare.

Answers:

Pages 11–12

1. (a) (ii) a river bank
   (b) The ant took a drink because it was a hot day and he was thirsty.
   (c) The little ant fell in the river because his feet slipped on a wet rock.
   (d) 1 The ant fell in the river.
       2. The dove noticed the ant was in danger.
       3. The dove dropped a leaf in the water.
       4. A hunter got out a net to catch the dove.
       5. The ant bit the hunter on the leg.
       6. The dove flew away to safety.
2. (i) perched – settled or resting on something
   (ii) thirsty – needing a drink
   (iii) yelled – cried out loudly
   (iv) drown – to die from being underwater too long
3. If you are good to others, they will be good to you.

Page 13

1–3. Teacher check

Extension:

The ant and the dove is one of many of Aesop's fables. Other titles suitable for this age group include:

The wind and the sun	*The fox and the grapes*
The lion and the mouse	*The town mouse and the country mouse*
The dog and the shadow	*The hare and the tortoise*

THE ANT AND THE DOVE – 1

Read the fable.

One hot day, a little ant was crawling along a river bank.

'How nice and cool the water looks', the ant thought to himself. 'I think I'll take a drink'. The thirsty ant crawled down to the edge of the river. As he began to drink, his feet slipped on a wet rock and he fell in. The water began to sweep him away.

'Oh, somebody please help me,' the little ant cried out, 'or I will surely drown!'

A dove, who was perched on a branch overhanging the river, saw that the ant was in danger.

'I can help him', she thought. 'If I drop a leaf into the water, the ant can climb onto it. It will be like a little boat.'

So the dove dropped the leaf close to the ant and called out what to do. The ant climbed onto the leaf and soon floated safely to the shore.

'Thank you, kind dove', said the little ant. 'You have saved my life. I hope I can help you one day.'

A few days later, a hunter came by looking for birds to catch. He saw the dove resting on a branch and began to get out his net. However, the little ant had seen what the hunter was up to. He raced up to the hunter and bit him on the leg. The hunter yelled in pain. The dove heard the noise and flew away to safety. The hunter picked up his net and walked on.

'Thank you this time, little ant', cooed the dove. 'You did help me after all'.

❶ Right there

(a) Circle the correct answer.

One hot day, a little ant was crawling along ...

(i) | the edge of a stream. | (ii) | a river bank. | (iii) | on the edge of a pond. |

(b) Why did the ant take a drink?

____

____

THE ANT AND THE DOVE – 2

Use the text on page 11 to answer the questions.

❶ Right there

(c) Why did the little ant fall in the river?

____

(d) Use the numbers 1 to 6 to show the order of each event in the fable.

| ☐ A hunter got out a net to catch the dove. | ☐ The ant fell in the river. |

☐ A hunter got out a net to catch the dove.

☐ The ant fell in the river.

☐ The dove noticed the ant was in danger.

☐ The ant bit the hunter on the leg.

☐ The dove flew away to safety.

☐ The dove dropped a leaf in the water.

❷ Think and search

Use a dictionary to help you match each word to its meaning.

(a) perched   •   • cried out loudly

(b) thirsty   •   • settled or resting on something

(c) yelled   •   • to die from being underwater too long

(d) drown   •   • needing a drink

❸ On my own

The story of the ant and the dove is a fable. A fable is a story with a moral, which means it teaches us a lesson. What do you think the moral of this story is? Tick the best answer.

Don't go near water if you can't swim.   ☐

If you are good to others, they will be good to you.   ☐

Bite people if you want to scare them.   ☐

Always use a boat on a river.   ☐

THE ANT AND THE DOVE – 3

Use the text on page 11 to complete the activities.

1 Explain how the dove helped the ant from possibly being drowned.

____

____

____

____

____

2 List two other ways the dove could have helped the ant.

(a) _______________________________

____

____

(b) _______________________________

____

____

3 Choose one of your answers to Question 2 to change part of the fable of *The ant and the dove*. Use your own words to fill in the missing lines. Draw a picture in the space below to illustrate how the dove helped the ant in your story.

... 'Oh, somebody please help me,' the little ant cried out, 'or I will surely drown!' A dove, who was perched on a branch overhanging the river, saw that the ant was in danger.

'I can help him', she thought. 'If I

____

____

____

So the dove _______________________________

____

____

____

King Arthur

Teacher information

Genre:

Legend

Question types and comprehension strategies:

- Analyses and extracts information from a legend to answer literal, deductive and evaluative questions.
- Makes connections based on prior knowledge, research and the text.
- Synthesises information to add specified features to an illustration.

Worksheet information:

- Before completing page 17, pupils should understand that:
    - Although many legends are told as if they are historical fact, this is not necessarily true.
    - For years, historians have attempted to establish a factual base for the Arthurian legends and continue to debate the issues today.
    - These stories have excited the imagination and have possibly guided the behaviour of people over many years.

Answers:

Pages 15–16

1. (c) and (e)
2. (a) Their meeting place was a round table.
   (b) He didn't want to favour any particular knight by having him seated at the top of the table.
   (c) They told each other stories about their great deeds before they could eat.
   (d) Teacher check
3. Teacher check

Page 17

Teacher check

Extension:

- Read and discuss stories about the adventures of King Arthur and his knights.
- Discuss the character and deeds of Sir Lancelot.
- Research to list characters from the Arthurian legends.

KING ARTHUR – 1

Read the legend.

There are many stories told about King Arthur and his knights of the round table.

Before Arthur was born, his father promised a man of mystery and magic called Merlin that he could bring up his first son. His father kept his promise and gave Merlin his baby son. Merlin gave Arthur to Sir Ector, whose wife looked after him very well.

When Arthur was a young man his father, the king, died. It was said that only the true king would be able to pull an old sword called 'Caliburn' out of the rock where it stood. The person to do this would be its rightful owner. Many strong men tried but they couldn't remove the sword. With Merlin's help, Arthur pulled out the sword and became king.

Only the strongest and best knights came to serve King Arthur. They became famous for their great deeds and courage.

The knights sat at a round table so they wouldn't be jealous of the knight chosen to sit at the head of the table.

No-one at the table could eat until each knight had told a story about something brave or good that he had done. The knights all tried to be the best.

One quest that all the knights were keen to follow was the search for the Holy Grail. This was the cup they believed Christ used at the Last Supper.

During one of the many battles Arthur fought, his sword was broken. Merlin took him to The Lady of the Lake who gave him a very special sword called 'Excalibur'.

No-one knows if the stories about King Arthur are true or even if there really was a King Arthur, but the stories about him and his knights have inspired people for hundreds of years.

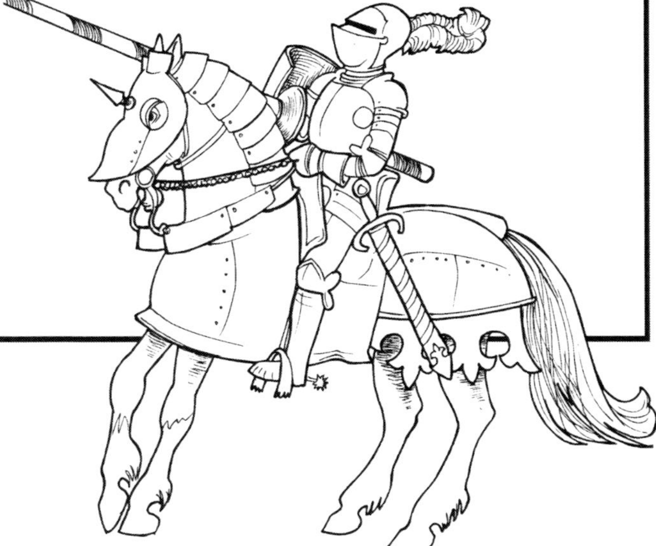

❶ Right there

Underline the correct answers.

(a) Sir Ector was Arthur's real father.

(b) 'Excalibur' was stuck in a rock.

(c) Merlin helped Arthur.

(d) Merlin gave Arthur a sword.

(e) Arthur broke 'Caliburn'.

(f) The Lady of the Lake was mean.

KING ARTHUR – 2

Use the text on page 15 to answer the questions.

Use the text on page 15 to answer the questions.

❷ Think and search

(a) Why were Arthur's knights called 'the knights of the round table'?

____

____

(b) Why did King Arthur want them to sit at a round table?

____

____

(c) What did the knights do at the round table to encourage each other to be good and brave?

____

____

____

(d) Draw what Arthur had to do to become king.

❸ On my own

(a) Why do you think many young men wanted to join King Arthur?

____

____

____

(b) Why do you think the knights wanted to find the Holy Grail?

____

____

____

____

Primary comprehension

KING ARTHUR – 3

1 Draw and label each piece of equipment used by knights to fight or to protect themselves in battle.

> sword, shield, helmet, gauntlets, lance, shoulder guards, breastplate, thigh guards, boots, spurs

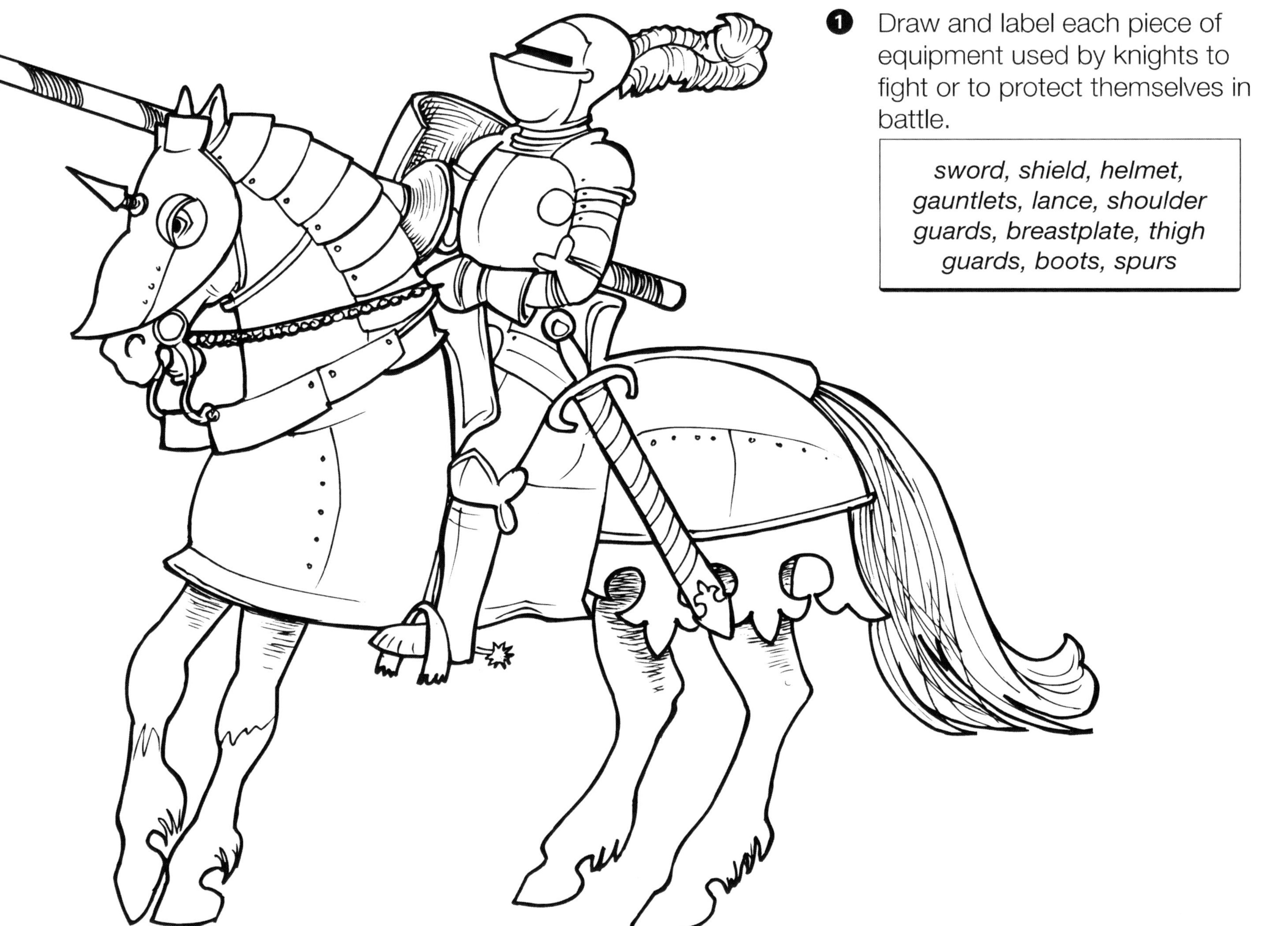

GAVIN, THE GENTLE GIANT

Teacher information

Genre:

Fractured fairytale

Question types and comprehension strategies:

- Analyses and extracts information from a fractured fairytale to answer literal, deductive and evaluative questions.
- Compares a fractured fairytale with the traditional version.
- Determines important information from a text to answer questions.

Worksheet information:

Fractured fairytales are often told from the point of view of another character. They may be based upon the original fairytale to some extent, but allow the author to change or extend events and characters to suit himself/herself.

Answers:

Page 20

1. (a) ... people were scared of him; he sometimes lost friends because he accidentally stepped on them.

    (b) ... his singing harp and hen that laid golden eggs.

    (c) ... work in the bean field.

2–3. Teacher check

Page 21

1–2. Teacher check

Extension:

Other fractured fairytales which pupils may enjoy reading or listening to include:

Prince Cinders by Babette Cole

Princess Prunella and the purple peanut by Margaret Atwood

The frog prince continued by Jon Scieszka

GAVIN, THE GENTLE GIANT – 1

Read the fairytale.

Once upon a time in a land in the clouds lived a giant called Gavin. He grew his crops of beans and sold them for gold coins. He used some of his gold to buy a harp that sang and a hen that laid golden eggs.

Unfortunately, Gavin didn't have many friends. People were often too scared to come close to him. If they did get to know him, it was often difficult for Gavin to keep them as he occasionally stepped on them by mistake. Gavin was a gentle, but lonely, giant!

One day, the face of a boy appeared at the top of the beanstalk. At first he was too scared to come near, but Gavin showed him his singing harp and the hen which laid the golden eggs. The boy, Jack, soon became a frequent visitor to Gavin's house.

'At last,' Gavin thought, 'I have a best friend of my own!'

Gavin even made a special set of bells for Jack to wear whenever he came to visit — just in case Gavin didn't know where he was and accidentally stepped on him!

One cold day when Jack came to visit, Gavin was making hot cocoa. As quick as a wink, Jack snatched the singing harp and the hen and scrambled down the beanstalk. When Gavin discovered his friend and his treasures gone, he wept huge tears which flowed out of the clouds and down the beanstalk. Jack was swept from the beanstalk and the treasures were washed from his hands. Jack's mother caught them as they fell to the ground.

'There you are, you naughty child!' she cried. 'Now I know what you have been up to — taking what isn't yours! It looks like I have another of your messes to clean up!'

Jack's mum locked him in his room to recite his times tables. Then she climbed the beanstalk with the harp and the hen tied up firmly in her apron.

When she reached the top of the beanstalk, she saw Gavin sleeping quietly on the lawn, exhausted by his tears. He awoke as she came near and she held out the harp and the hen as a sign of friendship.

'I'm sorry for what my son has done!' she said. 'I'll make sure that he is punished.'

Jack became a frequent visitor to Gavin's house again. He worked hard every day in the bean field while his mum and Gavin lived happily ever after, drinking cocoa and talking as good friends do!

GAVIN, THE GENTLE GIANT – 2

Use the text on page 19 to answer the questions.

❶ Right there

Complete the sentences.

(a) Gavin didn't have many friends because _________________

____

____

(b) While Gavin was making cocoa, Jack stole _________________

____

____

(c) Jack was punished by having to _________________

____

❷ Think and search

Write words to describe each character. At the bottom of each box, draw the face of each character.

Gavin	Jack	Jack's mother

❸ On my own

Often people we know do and say nasty things to us. Colour the words which would describe your feelings when this happens. You may colour more than one word.

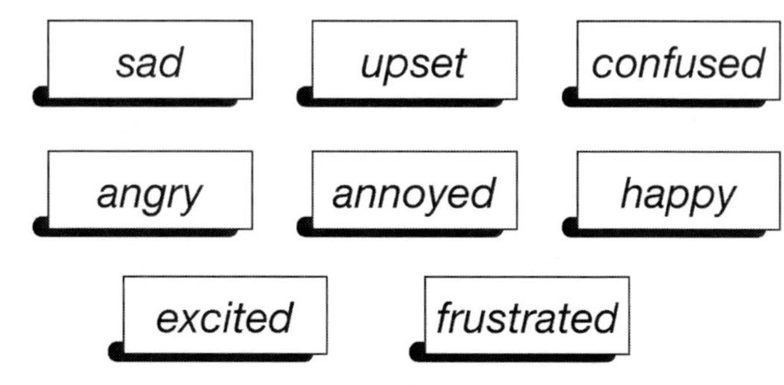

Primary comprehension

Prim-Ed Publishing   www.prim-ed.com

GAVIN, THE GENTLE GIANT – 3

Use the fairytale on page 19 to complete the activities.

1 Complete the table to compare this fairytale to *Jack and the beanstalk*.

Similarities

Differences

2 Write a sentence using information from the fairytale to answer the questions.

(a) Which incident showed Gavin that Jack was not his friend?

____

____

____

____

(b) How do you know that Jack got into trouble a lot?

____

____

____

____

(c) What things tell you that Jack's mother is a very capable person?

____

____

____

____

Genre:

Biography

Question types and comprehension strategies:

- Analyses and extracts information from a biography to answer literal, deductive and evaluative questions.
- Compares information in a text to his/her own experience.
- Makes connections between author and himself/herself.

Worksheet information:

Pupils could work in pairs or as a whole class and highlight the answers in the text to the questions about Beatrix Potter on page 25.

Answers:

Pages 23–24

1. (a) Hill Top Farm in the Lake District of England
   (b) Exploring the fields and woods, catching and taming wild animals, sketching and painting all they saw
   (c) (i) Benjamin Bunny   (ii) Squirrel Nutkin
       (iii) Tom Kitten   (iv) Mr Brock the badger
       (v) Jemima Puddleduck   (vi) Pigling Bland

2–3. Teacher check

Page 25

1–2. Teacher check

Extension:

- Pupils draw illustrated storymaps of Beatrix Potter stories.
- Choose a character from a Beatrix Potter story to describe in full and compare that character with his/her own character.
- Some Beatrix Potter stories include:

  The tale of Peter Rabbit
  The tale of Johnny Town Mouse
  The tale of Timmy Tiptoes
  The tale of two bad mice

Beatrix Potter – 1

Read the biography.

Children all over the world have grown up enjoying the stories of Peter Rabbit and all the other animals who live at Hill Top Farm in the Lake District of rural England. The creator of these stories was Beatrix Potter, who was born in London in 1866.

As a child, Beatrix and her younger brother, Bertram, spent their summer holidays in the peace and quiet of the Lake District, many miles from the hustle and bustle of the busy city. Here, they both discovered a love of nature. The two children spent their days exploring the fields and woods, catching and taming wild animals. They made many sketches and paintings of all they saw.

At home in London, Beatrix and Bertram had many unusual pets, including a hedgehog, a dormouse and even a pig which Beatrix bottle-fed. It followed her everywhere, sleeping at night in a basket beside her bed.

Beatrix wrote her first story, The tale of Peter Rabbit, *to cheer up a small boy named Noel, who was ill in bed. After some years, the story was published and it became one of the most famous stories ever written.*

Other animal characters include Benjamin Bunny, Tom Kitten, Jemima Puddleduck, Mrs Tiggywinkle, Squirrel Nutkin, Pigling Bland, Mr Brock the badger and Mr Todd the fox.

When Beatrix Potter married, she bought Hill Top Farm and dedicated her life to preserving the natural beauty of the Lake District. When she died in 1943, she left much of her land to the National Trust, an organisation which helps to preserve the beauty of many areas of the country for future generations.

❶ Right there

(a) Where do the characters of Beatrix Potter's stories live?

____

____

____

(b) How did Beatrix and Bertram spend their holidays?

____

____

____

BEATRIX **P**OTTER – **2**

Use the text on page 23 to answer the questions.

❶ Right there

(c) Complete these characters' names.

   (i)   Benjamin _______________

   (ii)   _______________ Nutkin

   (iii) Tom _______________

   (iv) Mr _______________, the badger

   (v)   Jemima _______________

   (vi) _______________ Bland

❷ Think and search

Why do you think Beatrix and Bertram enjoyed their holidays in the Lake District so much?

____

____

____

____

____

❸ On my own

(a) What problems do you think there might have been in the Potters' London home with Beatrix and Bertram's pet collection?

____

____

____

____

(b) Draw pictures of three unusual pets they had.

BEATRIX POTTER – 3

Use the text on page 23 to complete the activities.

❶ (a) Imagine you are Beatrix Potter. Answer the question in each box under her name.

(b) Answer the same questions about yourself.

	Beatrix Potter	You
Where do you live?		
Where do you spend your holidays?		
What are your hobbies?		
What pets do you have?		
What would you like to do when you are older?		

❷ What are the similarities and differences between you and Beatrix Potter?

Similarities	Differences

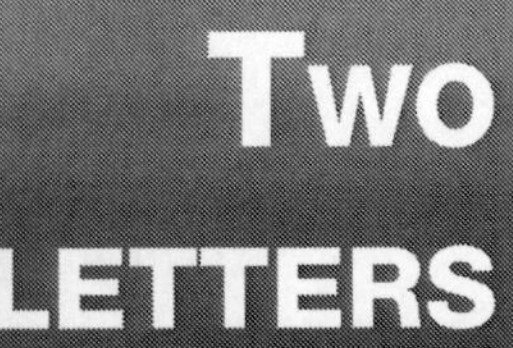

Teacher information

Genre:

Letter

Question types and comprehension strategies:

- Analyses and extracts information from a letter to answer literal, deductive and evaluative questions.
- Compares formal and informal styles of letter writing.
- Synthesises information from a text to determine its purpose and style.

Worksheet information:

Discuss when formal and informal letters are used and the formats required.

Formal letters – follow rules

- include personal information such as address, phone number, email
- formal ending such as 'Yours sincerely' or 'Yours faithfully'
- uses formal language ('have not' rather than 'haven't' etc.)
- no exclamation marks
- includes full names and the author's signature

Informal letters

- include first names
- can include shortened words (I'd, can't etc.)
- can use exclamation marks
- friendly style

Answers:

Page 28

1. (a) False (b) True (c) True (d) False (e) True
2. (a) For an appointment with the doctor.
   (b) They used to be at school together.
   (c) Sam has moved to a new school in another town.
3. Teacher check

Page 29

1. Letter 1: informal, friend, friend, Hi Sam, catch you later, alligator, Sarah, Yes, Teacher check, Teacher check
   Letter 2: formal, teacher, parent, Dear Mr Andrews, Yours sincerely, Mrs Robertson (mother), No, Teacher check, Teacher check
2. Teacher check

Extension:

- Read examples of formal and informal letters.
- Write formal letters for a purpose, such as requesting information from a company or organisation.
- Write informal letters to penpals in another school, city or country.

Read the letters.

Letter 1

Hi Sam

Haven't heard from you for ages! What have you been up to?

I can't believe I'm writing a 'snail mail'! It's such an old person thing to do! Why haven't you called me with your new phone number?

Life here is pretty good at the moment. We've got this great new teacher in school. She does lots of fun stuff, not like boring old Mr Johnson. Do you remember him?

We're off to the farm for the holidays again next week. I love it but it can be a bit b-o-r-i-n-g at night sometimes.

Please, please, please send me a phone number so I can call or text you. I hope all's going well in your new school. What's the town like?

Please get in touch and give me all your gossip!

Catch you later, alligator

Sarah

Letter 2

Dear Mr Andrews

Please excuse Robert from physical education this week as he has badly bruised the big toe on his left foot. He has been advised by the doctor to rest it for at least one week.

I would also like him to spend break times sitting quietly, close to the classroom if possible.

Robert has another appointment with the doctor on Friday afternoon. I will pick him up from school at the end of the morning session.

Thank you for your understanding.

Yours sincerely

Mrs Robertson (mother)

TWO LETTERS – 2

Use the letters on page 27 to answer the questions.

❶ Right there

Colour **true** or **false**.

(a) Mrs Robertson wrote to Sarah.

  TRUE   FALSE

(b) Sam is at a new school.

  TRUE   FALSE

(c) Sarah is going to the farm for the holidays.

  TRUE   FALSE

(d) Mr Andrews is the doctor.

  TRUE   FALSE

(e) Robert bruised his big toe.

  TRUE   FALSE

❸ On my own

(a) What do you think Sarah means by a 'snail mail'?

____

(b) Sarah's letter to Sam is a friendly, informal letter. What other phrases might she have used to introduce and sign off the letter?

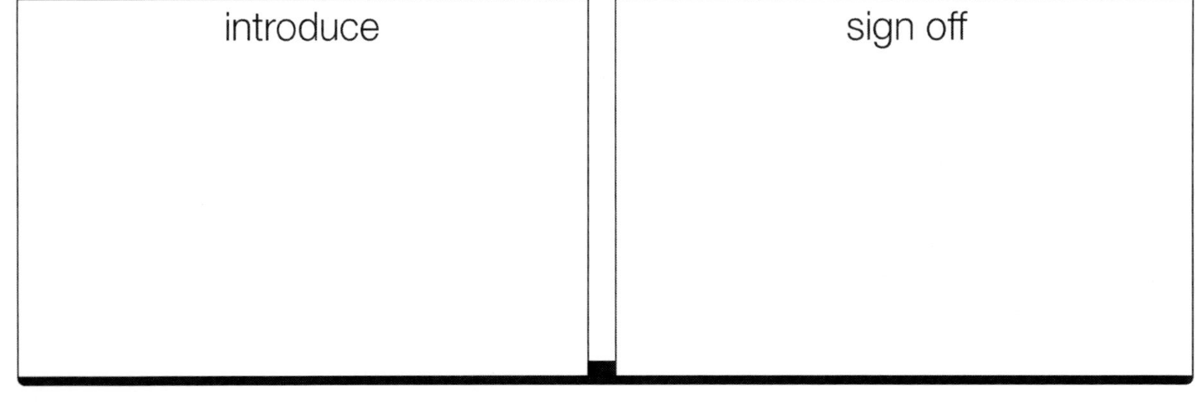

introduce	sign off

❷ Think and search

(a) Why is Robert leaving school early on Friday?

____

(b) How do Sam and Sarah know each other?

____

____

(c) Why don't Sam and Sarah see each other any more?

____

____

____

Primary comprehension   Prim-Ed Publishing   www.prim-ed.com

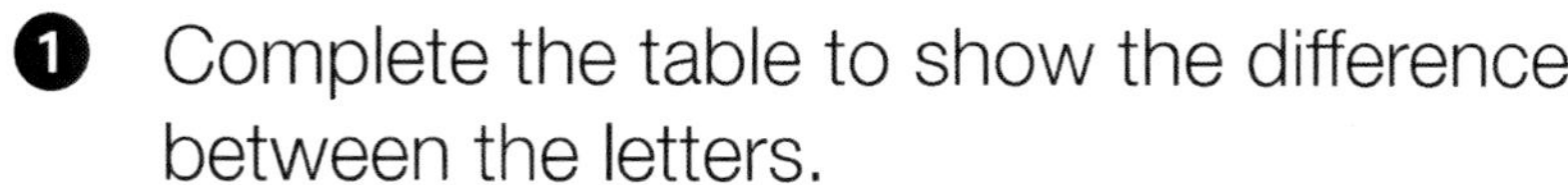TWO LETTERS – 3

Use the letters on page 27 to complete the activity.

1 Complete the table to show the difference between the letters.

	Letter 1	Letter 2
type – formal/informal		
Who was it written to? (friend, teacher etc.)		
Who was it written by? (friend, teacher etc.)		
What was the greeting at the start?		
How was the letter ended?		
Did it have exclamation marks?		
What kind of words were used?		
Why was it written?		

2 Give two reasons to write a formal letter and an informal letter.

Formal	Informal
• _______________	• _______________
_______________	_______________
• _______________	• _______________

Teacher information

Genre:

Fantasy

Question types and comprehension strategies:

- Analyses and extracts information from a fantasy text to answer literal, deductive and evaluative questions.
- Uses sensory imaging to describe a place.
- Scans a text to find specific words.

Worksheet information:

- A centaur is a mythical creature with the upper body of a human being and the lower body of a horse.
- A satyr is a mythical creature which is half man and half goat, with a beard and sometimes horns or goat's ears.
- The creature with the head of a lion, the body of a goat and the tail of a serpent was a chimera. In Greek mythology, the chimera is a monster, shown as an animal with the head of a lion, the body of a she-goat, and the tail of a dragon. Sometimes it has multiple heads. It terrorised Lycia (in Asia Minor), but was later killed by the Corinthian hero, Bellerophon.

Answers:

Page 32

1. (a) Green Mist Mountains (b) Darla (c) kind
   (d) he knew the creatures would accept him
2–3. Teacher check

Page 33

1–2. Teacher check
3. (a) said, shouted, echoed, gasped
   (b) Answers may include: centaur, troll, dwarf, satyr, witch, goblin
   (c) Teacher check
   (d) Answers may include: Cirrus, Green Mist Mountains, Darla, Thellon, Sevvy, Bera

Extension:

Pupils may enjoy listening to the following stories:
Pegasus, the flying horse by Jane Yolen *
Half magic by Edward Eager
Catwings by Ursula LeGuin

* Jane Yolen has written many books about mythical creatures which pupils may be interested in reading.

Read the fantasy.

Cirrus the centaur lived in the Green Mist Mountains with his parents, Thellon and Sevvy, far from the humans. The mountains were a magical place inhabited by creatures of all descriptions. The green mist hid the secret places where families of trolls, dwarfs, satyrs, witches and goblins lived and played.

Cirrus was popular with the other youngsters who lived on the mountain because he was funny and kind. His favourite companion was Darla, the dwarf. Cirrus would gallop through the hills and valleys with Darla clinging to his strong back as they visited their friends. Darla and Cirrus would amuse each other by telling 'clip, clop' jokes and limericks.

One day as Cirrus clambered over some rocks near the riverbed with Darla behind him, they heard moaning noises from a clump of bushes close by. Darla and Cirrus came to a sudden stop as the bushes rustled and swayed. A creature carefully rose from underneath. It was a very odd-looking creature with the head of a lion, the body of a goat and the tail of a serpent. Its face was weary but kind.

'Don't be scared!' the creature gasped. 'My name is Bera. I have travelled a long way to find the Green Mist Mountains. I am the last of my kind in the world. I only wish to find a peaceful place to spend my remaining days. I have heard that the creatures of the Green Mist Mountains are many and varied so will accept me as I am.' Darla and Cirrus led Bera from the river through the secret pathways into the Green Mist Mountains. A sea of unusual creatures greeted them as they reached the main clearing. Bera told his story and was allowed to settle in the forest. He kept to himself and didn't join any of the activities the other grownups did.

Cirrus, being the kind centaur that he was, decided to think of a plan to cheer up Bera. When the next full moon arrived, Cirrus coaxed Bera into the main clearing where a huge circle of fire blazed. He urged him to sit in a spot at the front of the other creatures. One by one, each creature or group of creatures came to the centre of the ring to show their talents. The trolls lifted heavy tree trunks high above their heads. The satyrs sped around the circle until a cloud of mist encircled everyone's heads. The blue witches performed vanishing tricks and the goblins sneaked into the crowd and revealed items they had taken without anyone noticing.

Cirrus was the last to appear.

'Clip, clop!' said Cirrus.

'Who's there?' said the crowd.

'Bera!' shouted Cirrus.

'Bera who?' echoed the crowd.

'Bera late than never!' said Cirrus.

A tiny smile lifted the corners of Bera's mouth.

Cirrus the Centaur's show – 2

Use the text on page 31 to answer the questions.

❶ Right there

Tick the correct word or words to complete each sentence.

(a) Cirrus lived with his parents in the

◯ *Blue Ridge Mountains.*   ◯ *Green Mist Mountains.*   ◯ *Red Desert Plains.*

(b) The name of Cirrus's best friend was

◯ *Bera.*   ◯ *Thellon.*   ◯ *Sevvy.*   ◯ *Darla.*

(c) The strange creature was

◯ *scary.*   ◯ *timid.*   ◯ *kind.*   ◯ *friendly.*

(d) Bera wanted to live there because

◯ *he thought he would find family there.*   ◯ *there were places to hide.*

◯ *he knew the creatures would accept him.*

❷ Think and search

(a) What do you think happened to the other creatures like Bera?

____

____

____

____

(b) Why do you think the creatures in the Green Mist Mountains accepted Bera so easily?

____

____

❸ On my own

Use the space below to write your own 'clip, clop' joke to tell to a friend.

Cirrus the Centaur's Show – 3

Use the fantasy on page 31 to complete the questions.

1 Use your imagination to write about the Green Mist Mountains.

I can see ...

I can smell ...

I can touch ...

I can hear ...

2 Write a sentence to show how you would feel to discover a creature from the Green Mist Mountains.

3 Scan the text to find and write:

(a) four words which mean 'different ways of talking'.

(b) the names of five imaginary creatures.

(c) four interesting adjectives.

(d) five names.

DON'T YOU DARE TELL

Teacher information

Genre:

Mystery

Question types and comprehension strategies:

- Analyses and extracts information from a mystery narrative to answer literal, deductive and evaluative questions.
- Uses sensory imaging to create appropriate background information for a mystery narrative text.
- Predicts likely events that could take place after the close of a mystery narrative text.

Worksheet information:

For page 37, the pupils could use their predictions to continue the mystery on page 35. They could also plan their own mystery by creating and answering a list of questions similar to those on page 37.

Answers:

Pages 35–36

1. (a) He was great at solving mysteries.
   (b) • small handwriting
       • grubby fingerprints
       • the name 'Tom' was rubbed into the paper
   (c) (i)   True
       (ii) False
       (iii) False
       (iv) True
       (v)   True

2–3. Teacher check

Page 37

Teacher check

Extension:

Other mystery stories the pupils might enjoy are:

Antonio S and the Mystery of Theodore Guzman – Odo Hirsch

Emily Eyefinger series – Duncan Ball

Encyclopedia Brown series – Donald J Sobol

DON'T YOU DARE TELL – 1

Read the mystery narrative.

'Who do you think left this for you?'

Ben frowned. 'I have no idea.'

I took the note from him and read it again.

Don't you dare tell my secret. If you do, you will be sorry. I will take your favourite things.

'I don't know any secrets!' Ben said. 'It's crazy. What should I do, Jeremy?'

Ben had come to me because I was great at solving mysteries. So far this term, I had worked out what had happened to Lucy's lunch money and Miss Spencer's silver pen. But this was more difficult. Ben had found the note on his desk after break with no sign of who might have left it.

'Let's look at the clues', I said. 'The handwriting is small, so it's someone older than us. And there's lots of grubby fingerprints, so it's someone who doesn't keep their hands too clean.' I peered at the note more closely. 'The person must have leant on the note to write something else. There's a name rubbed into it. It says … Tom. That's who we're looking for.'

'But there's heaps of boys called Tom at this school!' Ben wailed. 'How do we know which one it is?'

'I'll make a list of the most likely suspects', I said.

Over the next two days, I discovered there were only three boys called Tom at our school who were older than we were. All of them looked as if they would usually have dirty hands. Ben swore he had never spoken to any of them. I began to wonder if the note had been put on his desk by mistake. But on Friday, a toy that Ben had brought to school for newstelling disappeared from Miss Spencer's cupboard. In its place was another note.

I warned you not to tell anyone, but you didn't listen. Don't do it again.

❶ Right there

(a) Why was Ben asking Jeremy for help?

____

____

DON'T YOU DARE TELL – 2

(b)　List the three clues Jeremy found on the note.

(c)　Colour **true** or **false**.

(i)　The first note was left on Ben's desk.　TRUE　FALSE

(ii)　There was only one boy called Tom at Ben and Jeremy's school.　TRUE　FALSE

(iii)　Ben brought a silver pen to school for newstelling.　TRUE　FALSE

(iv)　The second note was found in Miss Spencer's cupboard.　TRUE　FALSE

(v)　Jeremy had found out what had happened to Lucy's lunch money.　TRUE　FALSE

❷ Think and search

(a)　Name two things that might make this mystery difficult to solve.

- ___________________________

- ___________________________

(b)　List words to describe the sort of person you think Jeremy is.

❸ On my own

Describe how you would you feel if you had received Ben's mysterious notes.

DON'T YOU DARE TELL – 3

Use the text on page 35 to answer the questions.

❶ Think about what might have taken place before the story begins by answering the questions below. You can be as creative as you like!

(i) Who do you think is leaving the notes for Ben?

____

____

(ii) What secret does he/she think Ben has found out?

____

____

(iii) Why does he/she think it is Ben who is telling the secret?

____

____

(iv) Who is really telling the secret?

____

____

❷ Consider your answers to Question 1 and the story on page 35 to help you predict what will happen next in the story. What steps do you think Jeremy will take to find the culprit? Will he succeed?

____

____

____

____

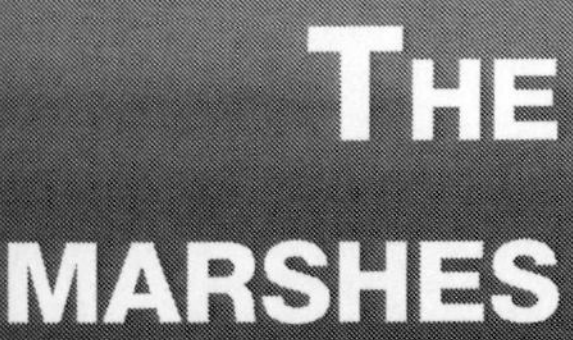

Teacher information

Genre:

Horror

Question types and comprehension strategies:

- Analyses and extracts information from a horror narrative to answer literal, deductive and evaluative questions.
- Uses sensory imaging to create emotional and visual images based on personal background knowledge and experiences.
- Predicts and explains events using the text and background information.
- Summarises text by identifying keywords.

Worksheet information:

- Pupils will benefit from opportunities to discuss their attitudes and feelings towards siblings and whether they believe these would change if someone was in extreme danger, before they complete page 40.
- On page 41, pupils are required to predict possible endings for the story and then to propose a positive solution to the character's problem. They should be encouraged to suggest realistic, believable solutions connected to the plot and setting of the narrative, rather than, for example, an alien rescue.

Answers:

Page 40

1. (b) is correct
2. (a) No   (b) Yes   (c) Yes   (d) Yes   (e) No
3. Teacher check

Page 41

1–3. Teacher check

Extension:

- Write a summary of the story based on the keywords selected.
- Create a collage by cutting out faces from magazines and gluing them in categories according to the feeling (emotion) pupils believe is reflected on each face.
- Write a character profile of a sibling detailing, for example, physical characteristics, personality, activities and likes and dislikes.

Read the horror story.

After days of miserable wet weather it was wonderful to see the blue sky. Dad decided the family should go for a drive into the country.

'Do we have to?' moaned Jan. 'It's so boring just driving and driving to nowhere and back again. I hate it.'

'Don't you complain. I have to put up with Dad's stupid music and Susie screaming her head off while you sit with headphones on doing nothing. You're selfish and mean and I hate you', her sister Bev added.

'Girls, girls can't you stop fighting just for a change?' Mum begged. 'We'll take a picnic lunch, you might even enjoy it.'

It seemed to take for ever, until Dad finally stopped the car. They all got out, unpacked the food and had lunch.

Susie ate everything she could get her hands on and fell asleep. Mum and Dad were comfortable in their chairs and obviously wouldn't be going home for a while. The two older girls decided to go for a walk.

After trudging along the track for a while, Jan thought it would be fun to cut across the marsh back to the main road and surprise Mum and Dad by coming back to the picnic spot from the opposite direction.

Bev thought it was a stupid idea, like most things her sister did, but she couldn't be bothered arguing. She followed Jan across the marsh.

'Yuk! It's horrible. Don't come this way I'm sinking', Jan complained.

Bev stopped and looked at her sister, who was up past her knees in the mud. 'I'm stuck, really stuck. I can't get out!'

As Bev watched, Jan seemed to be slipping down further into the sticky mud. She found a thin branch and told Jan to grab it. Sobbing, Bev pulled and pulled but Jan didn't move. She didn't want to leave, but she knew she had to get help fast.

Mum and Dad heard her yelling frantically as she came running up the track. They rushed to meet her and followed her back. When they got there, Bev screamed in horror. The branch was still there, but her sister was nowhere to be seen.

THE MARSHES – 2

Use the text on page 39 to answer the questions.

❶ Right there

Tick the correct one.

The family ...

(a) had a dog.

(b) went for a picnic.

(c) drove to the beach.

(d) all liked going for drives.

❷ Think and search

Colour **yes** or **no** after each question.

(a) The girls went for a walk in the rain.   YES / NO

(b) Susie was Bev's younger sister.   YES / NO

(c) Jan couldn't hear her father's music.   YES / NO

(d) Their parents were enjoying the picnic.   YES / NO

(e) The girls got on well together.   YES / NO

❸ On my own

(a) Which sister do you think is the oldest? _____________________ Why?

____

____

(b) Why was Bev sobbing as she tried to pull Jan out of the mud?

____

____

(c) Do you think Bev really hated Jan? _____________ Explain why you

think this. _______________________________________

____

THE MARSHES – 3

After reading the text on page 39, complete the activities.

1 (a) How do you think Jan was feeling when she realised she was stuck? Write words to describe her feelings.

(b) Draw Jan in the mud. Try to make your drawing show how she feels.

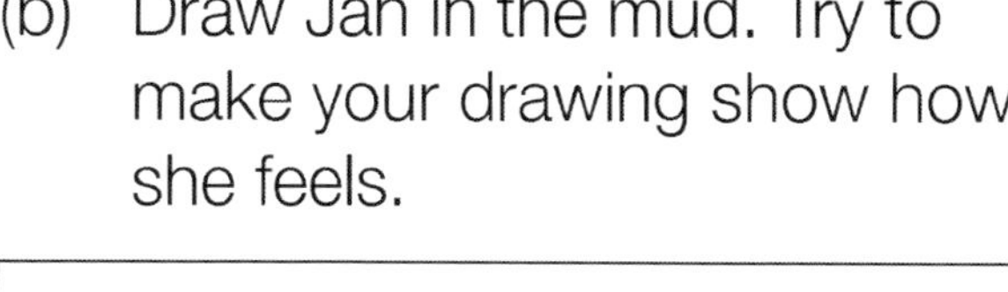

2 The story doesn't tell you what happened to Jan.

(a) What do you think happened? _______________________________

____

____

(b) Write a happy ending to the story. _______________________________

____

____

____

3 (a) Read *The marshes* again. Underline the keywords in the story. They should provide you with the main points for making a summary, which is a shorter form of the original story.

(b) Compare the keywords you underlined with a partner's keywords and decide if there are some more words you need to add or any words that you really don't need.

REMOTE CONTROL

Teacher information

Genre:

Film review

Question types and comprehension strategies:

- Analyses and extracts information from a film review to answer literal, deductive and evaluative questions.
- Uses sensory imaging to describe a character's experiences in a scene.
- Scans text to locate specific information.
- Predicts the ending of an adventure story.

Worksheet information:

Pupils could work in pairs or as a whole class to underline or highlight keywords and phrases to assist them to complete Question 1 on page 45. Question 2 could be completed individually or in pairs, before comparing endings with class members.

Answers:

Page 44

1. (a) Cale Cooper
   (b) 12
   (c) Blair Hunter
   (d) Simon Bergman
   (e) Jenny Jackson

2. (a) The DVD remote control has a part in controlling what happens in the film.
   (b) Answers could include: new hit, action-packed, nail-biting adventures, children get a thrill watching

3. Teacher check

Page 45

Teacher check

Extension:

- Pupils write a review and give a rating of up to five stars for a film they have watched.
- Daily newspapers include film reviews which can be read as a whole class and discussed.

REMOTE **CONTROL – 1**

Read the film review.

*Popular film director, Simon Bergman, has once again produced a blockbuster with his new hit, **Remote control**, starring 12-year-old Cale Cooper.*

In the film, Cale plays the part of Blair Hunter, who receives a DVD player for his birthday from his computer whiz relative, Uncle Lindsay. His uncle also includes a DVD for Blair to watch. As he settles down in a comfy chair and begins to watch it, to his surprise he realises that the main character in the film is actually Blair himself! He looks the same, sounds the same and even has the same name!

Blair finds that he is watching himself becoming involved in a series of adventures. In one scene, Blair is walking up a creaky staircase in what seems to be a castle. The wind is howling outside and is sneaking into the building through cracks and under doorways. Claps of thunder drown out the sound of the wind and lightning brightens up the dark house. Blair can make out furniture covered in dustsheets. Suddenly, at the top of the stairs, he sees a ghostly figure. Both 'Blairs' scream in fright. The Blair in the chair presses 'Stop' on the DVD remote control. When he has the courage to press 'Play' again, he finds himself in a different adventure!

The film continues with Blair discovering he can press the stop button to end the adventure and the play button to start another one. However, this changes when he decides to press 'Rewind'. Instead of the adventure changing, it goes back to where it ended. And this time 'Stop' will not work! No matter how scared he becomes, he is forced to watch.

***Remote control** will have cinemas packed during the school holidays as children get a thrill watching Blair's experiences. While the film is action-packed and involves many nail-biting adventures, it is still rated PG.*

My rating:

Jenny Jackson

REMOTE CONTROL – 2

Use the text on page 43 to answer the questions.

❶ Right there

Write a short answer for these.

(a) Who starred in the film? _______________________________

(b) How old is he? _______________________________

(c) What character did he play? _______________________________

(d) Who directed the film? _______________________________

(e) Who wrote the review? _______________________________

❷ Think and search

(a) Why is the film called *Remote control*? _______________________

____

____

(b) The film was given a score of four stars by the reviewer. Add words and phrases in the box alongside that the reviewer used to tell how good she thought the film was.

> *blockbuster*   *packed cinemas*

❸ On my own

(a) (i) After reading the review, do you agree that the rating should be PG?

YES ☐ NO ☐

(ii) Give a reason for your answer.

____

____

____

(b) Think of another title for this film.

____

REMOTE CONTROL – **3**

Use the text on page 43 to complete the activities.

1 Read paragraph 3 of the review. Use words and phrases from the text and your own imagination to describe Blair's experiences in the castle.

What Blair saw	What Blair heard

Blair's feelings

2 (a) Imagine Blair decided to press 'Rewind' instead of 'Stop' when he saw the ghostly figure in the castle so the adventure begins again from that moment. Describe what you think will happen next in the film and how the adventure might end.

____

____

____

____

____

____

(b) Share your ending with other class members.

Teacher information

Genre:

Play

Question types and comprehension strategies:

- Analyses and extracts information from a play to answer literal, deductive and evaluative questions.
- Makes connections between the features of a playscript and his/her own ideas to plan a new playscript with the same characters.
- Determines the importance of information in a playscript to plan his/her own playscript with the same characters.

Worksheet information:

When the pupils come to write their playscripts from page 49, teachers will need to discuss the structural conventions modelled in the playscript on page 47; e.g. a new line for each speaker, stage directions etc. Once written, the playscripts could be performed by small groups of pupils.

Answers:

Page 48

1. (a) She had moved perfectly, remembered all her lines and sung in tune.

   (b) Ethan tripped over on the stage and couldn't stop laughing, Amy forgot her lines and said silly things and David's guitar string broke, making his song sound weird.

2. (a) Teacher check

   (b) (iii) drama teacher

3. Teacher check

Page 49

1–2. Teacher check

Extension:

Look for plays adapted from popular children's books; e.g.

Charlie and the chocolate factory – Roald Dahl

The lion, the witch and the wardrobe – CS Lewis

Charlotte's web – EB White

THE SCHOOL PLAY – 1

Read the play.

Three children in school uniform, Amy, David and Ethan, are sitting outside a door. On the door is a sign that reads 'SCHOOL PLAY AUDITIONS TODAY'.

Amy	How much longer do you think Mr Dodd will be?
David	He said there was just Olivia left to audition. Then he said he'd tell the people waiting outside if they got a part in the play or not.
Ethan	I don't even know why I'm waiting. My audition was terrible. I tripped over on the stage. I couldn't stop laughing.
Amy	That doesn't sound any worse than my audition. I forgot my lines so I had to make them up. I said the silliest things!
David	You don't have anything to worry about. I decided to play my guitar and sing for my audition. But one of my strings broke and I had to play and sing without it! The song sounded really weird.
Ethan	It sounds like none of us has any hope of being in the play.
Amy	Let's go, shall we?

All three nod and stand up. Suddenly, the door opens and Olivia walks out.

David	How do you think you went, Olivia?
Olivia	**(tossing her head and smiling)** I was great! I moved perfectly, I remembered all my lines and I sang in tune. I'm sure to get a main role.

The door opens again. Mr Dodd steps out.

Mr Dodd	Is it just you four waiting to find out who got a part in the play?

They all nod.

Mr Dodd	Well, I'm happy to tell you that you were all successful. Congratulations!
Olivia	Is mine the main role?
Mr Dodd	No, I'm sorry, Olivia. I had to give the main roles to Amy, David and Ethan.
Ethan	What? Why would you give us parts? We all did terrible auditions. We were clumsy, we forgot our lines and we sang badly.
Mr Dodd	Yes, I know. You were perfect for this year's play. It's set at a circus … and the main characters are clowns!

Mr Dodd smiles, Amy, David and Ethan begin to laugh. Olivia stamps her foot and exits.

THE SCHOOL PLAY – 2

Use the text on page 47 to answer the questions.

❶ Right there

(a) Why did Olivia think she might have been given the main role in the play?

____

____

____

(b) List three things that went wrong in the auditions.

- ______________________________
- ______________________________
- ______________________________

❷ Think and search

(a) What sort of person do you think Olivia is? What makes you think this?

____

____

____

____

____

(b) Tick which job Mr Dodd is most likely to have.

(i) headteacher ☐

(ii) gardener ☐

(iii) drama teacher ☐

(iv) maths teacher ☐

❸ On my own

If you were Mr Dodd, would you have given the main roles to Amy, David and Ethan? Explain why/why not.

____

____

____

____

THE SCHOOL PLAY – **3**

Use the text on page 47 to help you complete this activity.

1 Imagine the auditions of Amy, David and Ethan. Plan a short playscript that describes what happened.

Beginning of playscript

- Playscripts often begin with a brief description of the setting.

  Describe the audition room and who is in it when your play begins.

  ____

  ____

  ____

- Who says the first line in your play? What does he/she say?

  ____

  ____

Middle of playscript

- Choose an audition piece for each character. It should be something you know well; e.g. a nursery rhyme, a favourite song.

  Amy   _______________________

  David   _______________________

  Ethan   _______________________

- Describe some of Mr Dodd's reactions to the auditions.

  ____

  ____

  ____

End of playscript

- Who says the final line in the play? What does he/she say?

  ____

  ____

- Playscripts often end with a description of the characters' reactions to the final line. Describe what the characters do at the end of your play.

  ____

  ____

2 Use the plan to help you write your playscript on a separate sheet of paper.

Teacher information

Genre:

Informational text (flow chart)

Question types and comprehension strategies:

- Analyses and extracts information from a flow chart to answer literal, deductive and evaluative questions.
- Scans visual and written text to determine importance of information.
- Summarises information by recording keywords and phrases from a flow chart.

Worksheet information:

Pupils could work in pairs to underline or highlight keywords and phrases on page 51 to assist them to summarise the story of milk production on page 53. The facts could be colour-coded according to the four headings on page 53.

Answers:

Page 52

1. (a) A cow is able to make milk after it has had a calf.

   (b) hay, water, grass, clover, grains

   (c) (i) A cow's udder has **four** teats.

       (ii) A cow needs milking **twice** a day.

       (iii) **Before** a cow is milked, the farmer washes its teats.

   2–3. Teacher check

Page 53

Teacher check

Extension:

Pupils could create their own flow charts, either individually, in pairs or small groups, for the following processes:

The story of bread ('From wheat to you')

The story of the recycling of a particular item

The story of how a letter gets to its destination

Look at and read the flow chart.

A cow makes milk after it has a calf. It can make up to 38 L of milk each day.

A cow needs to eat lots of food such as grass, clover, grains and hay to make good quality milk. It also needs to drink about 150 L of water each day.

Milk is stored in the cow's udder, which is like a large bag with four teats. A cow needs to be milked at least twice a day.

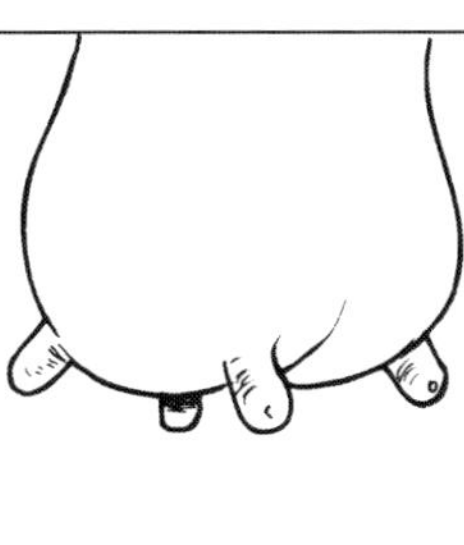

A refrigeration truck comes to pick up the milk daily and takes it to a special processing plant.

Before a cow is milked, the farmer washes its teats. A machine is put on the cow. The milk is pumped into large tanks and kept cool.

There it is tested and checked to make sure it is fresh and healthy.

The milk is quickly heated to 72° C for 15 seconds, to kill any bacteria (germs). This process is called 'pasteurisation'.

The milk is then forced through a sieve (a container with tiny holes) to break up any 'lumps' of fat. This process is called 'homogenisation'.

The milk is put into bottles or cartons and taken to the shops for us to buy. It can also be used to make other products such as butter, cream, ice-cream, cheese or yoghurt.

FROM THE COW TO YOU – 2

Use the text on page 51 to answer the questions.

❶ Right there

(a) When is a cow able to make milk?

____

____

(b) Circle the things a cow needs to make good quality milk.

hay	water	meat	grass
clover	bark	milk	grains

(c) The sentences below are incorrect. Rewrite each sentence so it is correct.

(i) A cow's udder has three teats.

____

____

(ii) A cow needs milking once a day.

____

____

(iii) After a cow is milked, the farmer washes its teats.

____

____

❷ Think and search

(a) Why are each of the following processes important?

(i) pasteurisation

____

____

(ii) homogenisation

____

____

(b) Circle and label the picture of a sieve you might use in a kitchen.

❸ On my own

Draw and label four milk products you like to use.

Use the flow chart on page 51 to complete the activity.

Write brief notes about the story of milk under each heading. Highlight or underline important words and phrases on page 51 before you write your answers.

What a cow needs to make milk	Description of where a cow stores milk
How a cow is milked	What happens to the milk at the processing plant

Teacher information

Genre:

Procedure

Question types and comprehension strategies:

- Analyses and extracts information from a procedure to answer literal, deductive and evaluative questions.
- Scans a text to find verbs.
- Synthesises the structure of a procedure to create his/her own procedure.

Worksheet information:

- Slime is an interesting substance because it acts like a solid and a liquid. When stress is placed upon it by stirring, pushing or pulling, it displays similar properties to a solid. When no pressure is placed on it, it will flow like a liquid.
- Look at other forms of instructional text such as recipes, board game instructions and instructions for building a household item and discuss their features.

Answers:

Page 56

1. (a) • Add food colouring to the mixture. [4]

    • Roll up your sleeves. [1]

    • Scrape around the sides of the bowl. [6]

    • Wrap the slime in plastic film. [10]

    • Throw the slime onto the board. [9]

   (b) (i) At step 5, you should stir the mixture until it becomes very hard to stir.

   (ii) You can add three to six drops of food colouring, depending on how green you would like your slime.

2–3. Teacher check

Page 57

1. Put, Add, Drop, Tip, Slap, Hold, Roll, Wrap
2. Teacher check

Extension:

Integrate literacy with science and use the instructions to make slime. Pupils can rate the instructions on a scale of 1 (easy to follow) to 10 (difficult/confusing to follow).

Note: Teachers are advised to try making slime prior to the activity as it will be easier to direct how much water to add.

<u>How to make slime – 1</u>

Read the instructions.

WHAT YOU NEED:

- *1 cup of cornflour*
- *3 to 6 drops of green food colouring*
- *an eye dropper (or small pouring jug)*
- *wooden board or chopping block*
- *water (in a container)*
- *plastic film*
- *mixing spoon*
- *mixing bowl*

WHAT YOU DO:

1 Put on your apron, roll up your sleeves and tie back your hair (if it is long).

2 Add the cornflour to the bowl.

3 Add drops of water to the cornflour VERY SLOWLY and mix it with the spoon.

4 Drop between three to six drops of green food colouring into the mixture (depending on how green you would like your slime.)

5 Add more drops of water to the mixture and stir it until it becomes very hard to stir.

6 Tip the slime out onto the board, scraping around the sides of the bowl.

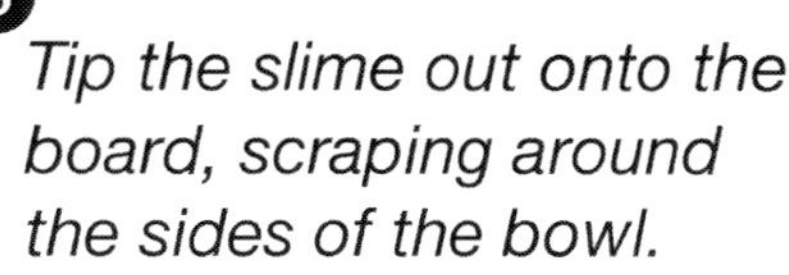

7 Slap the slime with your hand. It should feel hard like a solid object.

8 Hold the slime in your hand and open your fingers. Let the slime run through your fingers like a liquid. (If it doesn't, put it back in the bowl and add more water—not too much!)

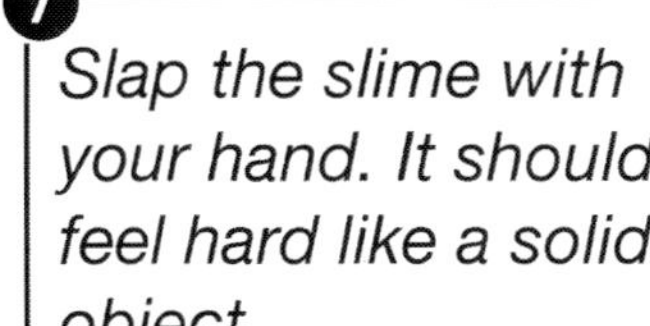

9 Roll the slime into a ball and throw it onto the board. What does it do?

10 Wrap the slime in plastic film and take it home. Impress your family with the mystery of your slimy creation!

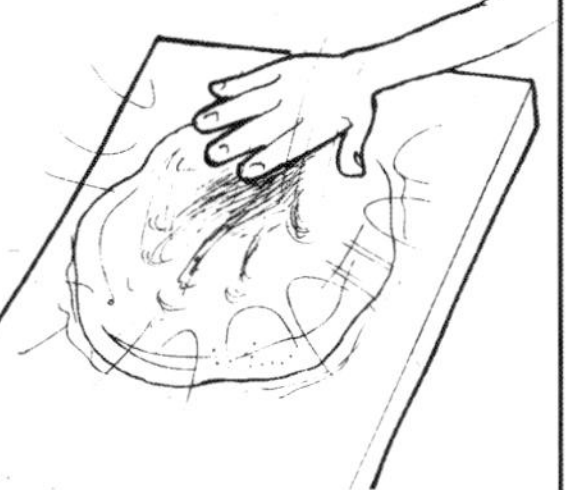

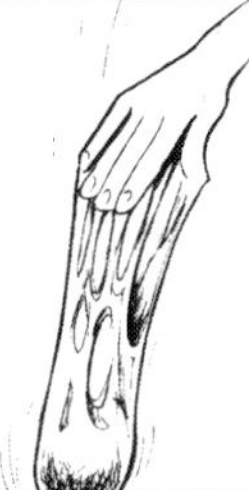

How to make slime – 2

Use the text on page 55 to answer the questions.

❶ Right there

(a) Write the number that matches the instruction.

- Add food colouring to the mixture. 
- Scrape around the sides of the bowl.
- Roll up your sleeves.
- Wrap the slime in plastic film.
- Throw the slime onto the board. 

(b) Finish these sentences.

(i) At step 5, you should stir the mixture until it ....

____

(ii) You can add three to six drops of food colouring, depending on ...

____

❷ Think and search

(a) Why should you wear an apron when making slime?

____

____

____

(b) Why do you think the words 'very slowly' are in capital letters in step 3?

____

____

____

❸ On my own

(a) Do you think you could follow these instructions to make slime?

| YES | NO |

(b) Why do you think the writer calls the slimy creation a 'mystery'?

____

____

____

Primary comprehension Prim-Ed Publishing   www.prim-ed.com

HOW TO MAKE SLIME – **3**

Use the text on page 55 to complete the activities.

1 A verb is a doing word. Texts that give instructions usually start with a verb. List the eight verbs that begin the instructions in 'How to make slime'. (Three are the same.)

_______________________________   _______________________________

_______________________________   _______________________________

_______________________________   _______________________________

_______________________________   _______________________________

2 Think of something that you know how to do. It could be making your breakfast, making your bed or setting the table. Write instructions for this. Start each one with a verb. Add some pictures.

How to _______________________________

1. _______________________________   2. _______________________________

_______________________________   _______________________________

3. _______________________________   4. _______________________________

_______________________________   _______________________________

Teacher information

Genre:

Humour

Question types and comprehension strategies:

- Analyses and extracts information from a humorous recount to answer literal, deductive and evaluative questions.
- Scans text to determine the order of events.
- Summarises information by recording keywords and phrases.
- Compares own reactions with the characters' reactions to situations in a text.

Worksheet information:

Pupils could work in pairs or as a whole class to underline or highlight keywords and phrases on page 59 to assist them in summarising each April Fool's Day joke on page 61. They could also discuss the answers to Question 3 on page 60 and compare what they think would be their reaction to each joke with each character in the text.

Answers:

Page 60

1. (a) four   (b) Sophie and Kelly
   (c) (i)   Dad – looked puzzled, then laughed
       (ii) Sophie – screamed, then went off in a huff
       (iii) Kelly – felt disgusted, then agreed it was a good trick
       (iv) Mum – giggled, and asked why she kept being tickled
2. (a) Teacher check
   (b) 1 April
   (c) Teacher check
3. Teacher check

Page 61

Teacher check

Extension:

Pupils could compile a list of April Fool's Day jokes to play on friends or family and illustrate each one. They should discuss the appropriateness of each before adding it to the list.

APRIL FOOL! – 1

Read the humorous recount.

Wow, what a day! My stomach is still aching from laughing so much. Now I know what the saying 'Laugh until your sides split' means! Today was a Saturday and it also happened to be April Fool's Day – 1 April. I had decided to play some April Fool's Day jokes on my family.

Firstly, it was Dad's turn. He always reads the newspaper first thing on a Saturday. I set my alarm for 6.30 am and fetched the paper from the porch. After carefully unrolling it, I swapped all the pages around. Then I rolled it up again and put it back in the porch for him to collect later. You should have seen the puzzled look on his face when he opened it! He turned it upside down and back to front. I popped out from behind the door and said, 'Look at the date on the paper, Dad!' He looked and started to laugh as I gleefully called out 'April fool!'

My younger sister was easy to fool. She fell for the 'plastic spider trick'. As she was about to sit at the table for breakfast I yelled, 'Sophie, watch out for that spider!' She screamed and jumped in the air. When I said 'April fool!', she went off in a huff back to her room. Dad and I laughed even louder.

Next it was my older sister's turn. In one hand I had a black beetle I found in the garden and in the other I had a black jelly bean. I showed Kelly the beetle, then swapped objects when she looked away. I put what she thought was the beetle in my mouth. 'You're gross, Jamie!' she said in disgust. But she admitted it was a great trick after I said, 'April fool!' and showed her the chewed jelly bean, and the beetle in my other hand.

To trick Mum, I stuck a note on her back that said 'Tickle me!' After being tickled a few times by each of us she giggled, 'Why does everyone feel like tickling me today?' She giggled even more when I exclaimed, 'April fool!'

But the jokes hadn't ended yet. Mum made some delicious hot chocolate for morning tea. I added a spoonful of sugar and took a sip. Yuk! I spat it back into the cup.

'April fool!' Mum laughed, as she showed me the salt packet and the 'sugar' bowl!

APRIL FOOL! – 2

Use the text on page 59 to answer the questions. 

❶ Right there

(a) Circle the number of people Jamie tricked on April Fool's Day.

five	**three**	**one**	**four**	**two**

(b) What were the names of Jamie's sisters?________________________

(c) Match what each person did when Jamie tricked him or her.

(i) Dad •   • screamed, then went off in a huff.

(ii) Sophie •   • giggled, and asked why she kept being tickled.

(iii) Kelly •   • looked puzzled, then laughed.

(iv) Mum •   • felt disgusted, then agreed it was a good trick.

❷ Think and search

(a) Explain what Jamie meant by the saying 'Laugh until your sides split'.

____

____

(b) What date would Dad have
seen on the paper?

____

(c) Explain how Jamie was tricked.

____

____

____

❸ On my own

Describe the trick you thought was the best and the reasons for your choice.

____

____

____

____

____

April Fool! – 3

Use the text on page 59 to complete the activities.

1 (a) Use keywords and phrases to describe each April Fool's Day joke. Make up a name for each—e.g. 'The plastic spider trick'—and list them in the order they happened.

(b) Next to each joke, write words to describe how you would have felt if the joke had been played on you; e.g. angry, puzzled, amused, scared.

Joke's name and description	My reaction
Joke 1 ___________________________	
Joke 2 ___________________________	
Joke 3___________________________	
Joke 4 ___________________________	
Joke 5 ___________________________	

JOJO, THE MONKEY

Teacher information

Genre:

Poetry

Question types and comprehension strategies:

- Analyses and extracts information from a poem to answer literal, deductive and evaluative questions.
- Scans a text to identify rhyming words.
- Synthesises the structure of a poem to write another poem with a similar theme.

Worksheet information:

Discuss the features of poetry. Ask the pupils to give examples of any poems they know by heart. How do they know them? Discuss rhyming words and give examples.

Answers:

Pages 63–64

1. (a) (i) two (ii) big (iii) Bubble
   (b) The daughters are missing great big clumps of hair.
   (c) Jojo rode around on the cat.
2. (a) Jojo came from the pet shop.
   (b)–(c) Teacher check
3. (a) Teacher check
   (c) fair, hair; that, cat; disaster, faster; Bubble, trouble

Page 65

Teacher check

Extension:

Read other poems that involve animals.

Poetry anthologies about animals include:

Alphabeasts by Dick King-Smith

Pet poems by Jennifer Curry

Alphabestiary: Animal poems from A to Z by Jane Yolen

Monkeys write terrible letters by Arnold Spilka

Animal lullabies by Pamela Conrad

Animals on parade by Sara Willoughby Herb and Steve Herb

JOJO, THE MONKEY – 1

Read the poem.

Jojo is a monkey
A cute, tiny ape
A monkey for a pet?
What a huge mistake!
Our two daughters
So sweet and fair
Are missing great big
Clumps of hair!
Oh my goodness!
Jojo! STOP THAT!
You can't go riding
On the cat!
Boom! Bang! Crash!
Our home is a disaster!
Back to the pet shop
Faster! Faster!
Jojo we swapped
For a fish named Bubble.
He eats and swims
And is never any trouble.

❶ Right there

(a) Circle the correct answer.

   (i) How many daughters are there?

one	two
three	four

   (ii) Which word does not describe Jojo?

cute	big
monkey	tiny

   (iii) What is the name of the fish?

Cuddle	Trouble
Muddle	Bubble

(b) What are the daughters missing?

____

____

____

(c) What did Jojo do to the cat?

____

____

____

Jojo, the monkey – 2

Use the text on page 63 to answer the questions.

❷ Think and search

(a) Where did Jojo the monkey come from?

____

(b) Who did you think is 'speaking' in the poem? ____________________

Why do you think this? ________________________________

____

(c) How do you think the family were feeling when …

they first brought Jojo home?	*Jojo was riding the cat?*	*they brought Bubbles home?*

❸ On my own

(a) Who would you rather have as a pet? | Jojo | | Bubbles |

Explain your choice. ____________________________________

____

(b) *Jojo the monkey* is a rhyming poem. The last word in 'line 2' and 'line 4' of each stanza rhyme (or almost rhyme).

For example:

Stanza 1:	
Line 1 Jojo is a monkey	(doesn't rhyme)
Line 2 A cute, tiny **ape**	(rhymes)
Line 3 A monkey for a pet?	(doesn't rhyme)
Line 4 What a huge **mistake!**	(rhymes)

(c) List the four other pairs of rhyming words in the poem.

__________   __________

__________   __________

__________   __________

__________   __________

JOJO, THE MONKEY – 3

Use the text on page 63 to help you complete this activity.

The family in the poem had a terrible time when they brought Jojo home from the pet shop. Imagine you have brought an unusual pet home to your house that causes a problem.

❶ Plan a poem about this pet.

Type of animal:	Pet's name:

What does the pet do to make you take him or her back to the pet shop?

❷ Write your poem. Make the words at the end of line 2 and line 4 rhyme.

Line 1 ________________________ is a ________________________

Line 2 ____ (rhyme)

Line 3 ____

Line 4 ____ (rhyme)

Line 1 ____

Line 2 ____ (rhyme)

Line 3 ____

Line 4 ____ (rhyme)

❸ Draw a picture of your pet causing trouble.

Teacher information

Genre:

Report

Question types and comprehension strategies:

- Analyses and extracts information from a report to answer literal, deductive and evaluative questions.
- Scans a report to find relevant information to complete a fact file.
- Uses synthesis to complete a fact file about an animal.

Worksheet information:

Once the pupils have completed their fact files on page 69, a class discussion could be held about different endangered animals, what can be done to help them and which are most at risk.

Answers:

Pages 67–68

1. (a) They fly high in the air and they don't often come to the ground.

     (b) (i) 3   (ii) 30

          (iii) 2   (iv) 4

     (c) The pipe vine leaves have made it poisonous.

     (d) They both have bright yellow bodies and red markings on their wings.

2. Teacher check

3. Teacher check

Page 69

Teacher check

Extension:

Collect other animal reports from encyclopedias and the Internet. Discuss the kind of information they contain.

GIANT **BUTTERFLY – 1**

Read the report.

Do you know which is the largest butterfly in the world? It is the Queen Alexandra's birdwing butterfly. The wingspan of the female butterfly can be up to 30 centimetres long. That's the length of a ruler!

This amazing animal lives in a small area of rainforest in Papua New Guinea. Like all butterflies, it begins life as an egg. This is laid by the female Queen Alexandra's birdwing on only one type of plant – the pipe vine. It then takes four months before the egg becomes a butterfly. First, a caterpillar hatches from the egg. The caterpillar then eats the leaves of the pipe vine until it is ready to make a cocoon. Inside the cocoon, it changes into a butterfly. The Queen Alexandra's birdwing butterfly usually lives for about three months. It is not often eaten by predators. One reason for this is that the pipe vine leaves eaten by the caterpillar are poisonous.

Male and female Queen Alexandra's birdwings look different from each other. The males are smaller and have black wings with yellow, blue, green and red markings. The females have dark brown wings with cream and red markings. Both the male and female butterflies have bright yellow bodies.

Queen Alexandra's birdwings like to fly high in the air where they feed on the nectar of flowers. They don't often come to the ground. This can make it difficult to find out how many there are. But it is known that they are endangered. This is mainly because large areas of their rainforest home have been cleared of trees by people for farming and houses. Some people also catch and sell the butterflies for large sums of money. This is against the law.

The government of Papua New Guinea is trying to save the butterfly by helping people to set up butterfly farms, protecting areas of the rainforest from logging and planning to grow the pipe vine in different habitats.

❶ Right there

(a) What makes it difficult to find out how many Queen Alexandra's birdwing butterflies there are?

____

____

Giant Butterfly – 2

❶ Right there

(b) Number quiz

    (i)   How many months does the adult butterfly live for?

    (ii) How many centimetres long can the butterfly's wingspan be?

    (iii) How many different coloured markings are found on the female butterfly's wings?

    (iv) How many months does it take before the egg becomes a butterfly?

(c) Why is the adult butterfly not often eaten by predators?

____

____

____

(d) List the things the male and female butterflies have in common.

❷ Think and search

(a) What do you think is meant by the word 'wingspan'?

____

(b) What might be one reason the male butterfly is more brightly coloured than the female?

____

____

❸ On my own

Do you think it should be illegal to catch and sell endangered animals? Explain why/why not.

____

____

GIANT BUTTERFLY – 3

Create a fact file using the information from the report on page 67.

Fact file

Name

Appearance of adults

Habitat

Stages of life cycle

What do the adults eat?

Adult habits

Problems for this animal

Suggested solutions

How important do you think it is to help this animal? Why?

Teacher information

Genre:

Newspaper article

Question types and comprehension strategies:

- Analyses and extracts information from a newspaper article to answer literal, deductive and evaluative questions.
- Uses synthesis to imagine himself/herself in the role of a television reporter.
- Uses prediction to write a television news story.

Worksheet information:

- For page 73, the pupils could write complete television news reports and perform them for the class or a small group.
- The pupils could try creating a labelled picture of what they think the dinosaur might have looked like.

Answers:

Pages 71–72

1. (a) The 'soarosaurus' is a flying dinosaur with wings about the length of a bus and a body about the size of an elephant's.

   (b) They are busy digging for more bones.

   (c) Answers will vary, but should include the following: the archaeologists have not yet shown the full skeleton; the photographs of the leg bones could be from a number of different dinosaurs; it is surprising that something the size of an elephant could fly; the team might want to become famous or make money; the photographs were very blurry.

2. Teacher check

3. Teacher check

Page 73

   Teacher check

Extension:

Collect articles from newspapers and the Internet. Use them as examples to help the pupils write their own articles.

DINOSAUR FIND – 1

Read the newspaper article.

AUSTRALIAN DINOSAUR CLAIM

The remains of an unusual dinosaur may have been found in Australia—if a team of archaeologists is to be believed.

The team claims to have found the complete skeleton of a flying dinosaur, which they have named 'Soarosaurus'.

'Our find will astound the world', said a member of the team yesterday. 'The dinosaur is the most enormous animal that has ever flown. Its wings are about the length of a bus and its body is the size of an elephant's.'

Although the news of the find has many scientists buzzing with excitement, others are sceptical, saying they will 'believe it when they see it'.

'The archaeologists have yet to show the full skeleton to the world', says Professor Kent Binnings of Carleton University. 'So far, I have only seen photographs of a few leg bones, which could be from a number of different dinosaurs. I would be very surprised if something the size of an elephant could fly.'

Well-known archaeologist Sandra Green agrees, suggesting that the Australian team is either mistaken or playing some kind of joke. 'The idea of this dinosaur existing is ridiculous', she says. 'I suspect the team just wants to become famous or make money. The photographs of the dinosaur I was shown were very blurry and could have been of any large bones.'

The team have refused to show any more photographs, saying that they are too busy digging for more bones in the secret location where they claim the skeleton was found.

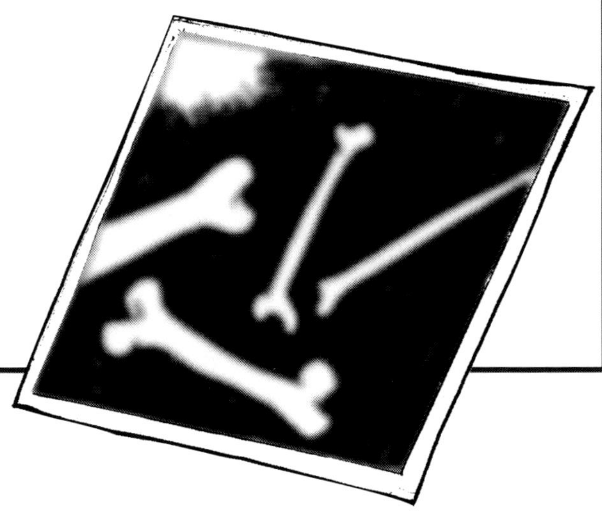

❶ Right there

Use the text to answer the questions.

(a) Describe the dinosaur the archaeologists claim to have found.

____

____

DINOSAUR FIND – **2**

❶ Right there

(b) Why does the team say it has not taken more photographs?

____

____

____

(c) List three reasons why Binnings and Green find it hard to believe the archaeologists.

❷ Think and search

(a) Choose another suitable name for the Soarosaurus.

____

(b) Explain why you chose it.

____

____

____

(c) Do you believe the archaeologists? Why/Why not?

____

____

❸ On my own

Imagine that the world's most amazing dinosaur find happens tomorrow. Write a list of reasons why it is so amazing.

DINOSAUR FIND – **3**

Imagine you are a television news reporter. You read the article on page 71 and decide to find out if the archaeologists are telling the truth. You discover the secret location and arrive there unnoticed.

1 Describe what you think you will see.

2 Before anyone notices you, write three questions to ask the team.

3 A member of the team discovers you. She is angry but agrees to talk to you. Write what you think she will answer for each of your questions.

-
-
-

4 You return to work to write a report for the news that night. Write the opening three or four sentences of your report below.

Teacher information

Genre:

Diary

Question types and comprehension strategies:

- Analyses and extracts information from a diary entry to answer literal, deductive and evaluative questions.
- Summarises information about a character from a diary entry.
- Predicts a future diary entry for a character based on the information gained from an earlier entry.

Worksheet information:

- *Myrmecia* (mer-me-she-a) is the scientific name for the bull ant.
- For page 77, the pupils may like to write a complete diary entry or narrative that details the next events in Myrmecia's life.
- The pupils may like to write a diary entry for another small creature, after researching some facts about its environment, physical features, social behaviour etc.

Answers:

Page 76

1. (a) hundreds
    (b) (i) She knew that she would find plenty of crumbs and other tasty treats.
         (ii) The queen was ill and the extra food would make her better.
         (iii) She was afraid of falling.
2. Teacher check
3. Teacher check

Page 77

Teacher check

Extension:

Other suggested diary titles:

The diary of a young Roman girl by Moira Butterfield

Penny Pollard's diary by Robin Klein

Royal diaries series by various authors (Scholastic)

Read the diary entry.

Dear diary

Today has been so terrifying I can hardly bring myself to write about it. It began like any other day. I woke up early and scurried off to meet the hundreds of other worker ants. When I arrived, they were talking about the queen.

'She is ill', I heard one of them say. 'We need to find extra food today to help make her better.'

I could hardly believe my antennae! Our queen, not well? This could mean disaster for the colony. Straightaway, I raced out of our rotten log home and into the picnic ground. I knew the best place to find food—under the picnic table. There were always lots of breadcrumbs and other tasty treats there.

I am usually very careful about watching where I am going, but today, I was thinking so hard about getting the food that I forgot to look out for our worst enemy—humans. It was only when the sky went dark that I looked up and realised that the sole of a human shoe was about to stomp on me.

I only had a split second to decide what to do. I couldn't stay on the ground so I ran up the human's bare leg. I was glad that he was wearing shorts. Trousers and jeans are so difficult to race up quickly! I ran up to his knee and paused for a moment. I didn't want to go any higher—I was afraid of falling. I got so worried that before I knew it, I bit the human's leg.

'Ow!' His hand darted towards me. I gulped and just managed to duck out of the way.

'James! Time to go!'

The human started to walk so I clung on as best I could, trying not to move. I knew that if he felt me, he would try to slap me again. He arrived at a car and got in. As soon as he slammed the door, the car started moving. I made my way onto the rough carpet, trembling and shaking. I hid under the front seat and stayed there until the car stopped moving and the humans got out.

Now I am stuck here! There is no food and I don't know where I am. I'll have to find a way out tomorrow. Will I ever see home again?

Myrmecia

DIARY OF AN ANT – 2

Use the text on page 75 to answer the questions.

❶ Right there

(a) How many ants does Myrmecia work with? _______________________

(b) Why:

  (i) does Myrmecia head for the picnic table? _______________________

  ____

  (ii) did the worker ants need to find extra food? _______________________

  ____

  (iii) didn't Myrmecia want to climb too high? _______________________

  ____

❷ Think and search

Give two reasons why it might be difficult for an ant to run up trousers quickly.

❸ On my own

Imagine this diary entry is going to be made into the opening scenes of an animated film. Draw three film frames that show the most exciting parts of the diary entry. Add a caption for each frame.

DIARY OF AN ANT – **3**

Use the text on page 75 to help you complete this page.

Myrmecia's diary ends with her shut in the car. What do you think might happen to her the next day?

1 Begin by listing the information you have learnt about her so far.

Home	Job

Things she is good at/likes to do	Things she is not as good at/doesn't like to do

Other details

2 Use the information to write the first four to five sentences of Myrmecia's next diary entry.

Dear diary

____

____

____

____

____

____

____

HALVAR'S HOUSE

Teacher information

Genre:

Folktale

Question types and comprehension strategies:

- Analyses and extracts information from a folktale to answer literal, deductive and evaluative questions.
- Creates a summary of a folktale by completing details of its setting, characters and main events.
- Scans a folktale to find relevant information about the setting, characters and events.
- Uses sensory imaging to draw imagined pictures of events contained in a folktale

Worksheet information:

For page 81, the opinions of the characters' behaviour could be used as the basis for a simple debate; e.g. 'Halvar should not have helped the man', 'One good turn deserves another'.

Answers:

Page 80

1. (a) He gave most of what he had to others.

   (b) His farm was not doing well.

   (c) (i) Answers will vary but may include the following: she was so skinny her ribs stuck out; the man wanted to sell her at the market; or Halvar swapped her for seven goats.

   (ii) Answers will vary but may include the following: they appeared in the farmer's barn in place of the cow; they gave the man more milk than he could ever drink; or they made the man very rich.

   (iii) It was beautiful or it was being ridden by the man.

2–3. Teacher check

Page 81

Teacher check

Extension:

Collections of folktales from around the world can be found in the following books:

Folktales and fables series by Robert Ingpen and Barbara Hayes

Rich man, poor man, beggarman, thief: folk tales from around the world by Marcus Crouch

The young Oxford book of folk tales by Kevin Crossley-Holland

Halvar's house – 1

Read the folktale from Sweden.

Once there was a giant called Halvar. He lived in a huge stone house in the hills. Halvar was a very poor giant because he gave most of what he had to others. This made him happy.

One day, Halvar was sitting outside his house when a man came past, leading a cow. The man was wearing ragged clothes. The cow was so skinny that Halvar could see its ribs sticking out.

'Hello', the man called out to Halvar. 'Can you tell me if this road leads to the markets?'

'Yes it does', said Halvar. 'Are you hoping to sell your cow?'

'Yes', said the man. 'Although I'm not too hopeful. You can see how thin she is. But I have no choice. My farm is not doing well and I need to eat.'

Halvar felt sorry for the man. 'I would like to help you', he said. 'Go home and put your cow back in the barn. In the morning, you will find seven goats in her place.'

The man could hardly believe his ears. But he had heard of Halvar's kindness and decided to take a chance. He walked back home and put the cow in the barn.

The next morning, the man opened the barn door to find seven goats instead of the cow. From that time on, life got much better for the man. The goats gave him more milk than he could ever drink. He made some of the milk into cheese and sold it for a good price at the market. Soon, the man became very rich and forgot all about Halvar. Then one day, he passed by Halvar's house again. This time, he was riding a beautiful horse.

'Hello', Halvar called out. 'Come and chat to me for a while.'

'I haven't got time', said the man. 'Don't you know that I'm an important man in the village now?'

Sadly, Halvar watched the man ride away. But then he remembered how much he enjoyed giving things away and making people happy. He kept on being kind to others no matter how they treated him.

Today, Halvar's house still stands in the hills of Sweden. It is a place where children love to play.

Halvar's House – 2

❶ Right there

(a) Why was Halvar poor?

____

____

(b) Why was the man poor?

____

____

(c) Write a fact about each type of animal in the story.

(i) cow _____________________

____

(ii) goats ___________________

____

(iii) horse ___________________

____

❷ Think and search

(a) Why do you think children might love to play in Halvar's house?

____

____

____

____

(b) Tick the best ending for the sentence.

The man didn't stop to talk to Halvar because

(i) he had a beautiful horse. ☐

(ii) he felt too busy and important. ☐

(iii) he didn't like Halvar. ☐

(iv) he didn't recognise Halvar. ☐

❸ On my own

Imagine the man had stopped to talk to Halvar. Write a new ending for the folktale.

The man got off his horse and spoke to Halvar.

____

____

Halvar's house – 3

Use the text on page 79 to help you complete this activity.

Make a summary of *Halvar's house* by completing the details below.

Setting

Describe what you think Halvar's house looks like.

Characters

Write the names of the two main characters in the story. Under each, write your opinion of the character's behaviour in the story.

Character 1

Opinion

Character 2

Opinion

Main events

Order the events below from 1 to 4. Draw a picture to show each event.

The man opened his barn door.

Halvar offered to help the man.

The man saw Halvar again.

The goats made the man rich.